RACQUETBALL

About the Authors

Dr. Philip E. Allsen, currently a professor of Physical Education at Brigham Young University, has been active in many aspects of physical education. He earned his B.S. at Ricks College, M.S. at Brigham Young University, and Ed.D. at the University of Utah. He has held positions at all three schools and has also served as athletic director for the city of Gardena, California, and as a Physical Fitness Officer in the U.S. Navy. Dr. Allsen has held his present position for the past 23 years. He holds honors and memberships in many professional organizations, ranging from the American College of Sports Medicine to the Nutrition Today Society. He is the author of over 100 professional articles. Besides coauthoring four editions of *Racquetball* for WCB, Dr. Allsen has also coauthored three other books published by WCB; *Fitness for Life, Physical Fitness and Conditioning: Current Answers to Relevant Questions,* and *Jogging.*

Professor Alan R. (Pete) Witbeck has been involved in racquetball as a teacher and outstanding player for the past 42 years. Professor Witbeck, who earned both his B.S. and M.S. degrees at Brigham Young University, has been a member of the faculty there for 36 years, presently serving as Associate Athletic Director. He has also compiled a successful coaching record at BYU. During 5 years as freshman basketball coach, his teams had an overall record of 62 wins and 9 losses, including one undefeated season. During the first 10 years of the Western Athletic Conference as varsity assistant, the BYU team won 5 championships. For his outstanding work in sports he has been given the prestigious Dale Rex Memorial Award, which is presented to the person who has contributed most to amateur athletics in the state of Utah.

Both authors are firm believers in physical conditioning for all ages and enjoy many sports in addition to racquetball.

RACQUETBALL

Sixth Edition

Philip E. Allsen

Brigham Young University

Pete Witbeck

Brigham Young University

Brown & Benchmark
PUBLISHERS

Madison, WI Dubuque Guilford, CT Chicago Toronto London
Mexico City Caracas Buenos Aires Madrid Bogotá Sydney

Book Team

Publisher *Bevan O'Callaghan*
Project Editor *Theresa Grutz*
Production Editor *Terry Routley*
Proofreading Coordinator *Carrie Barker*
Art Processor *Renee Grevas*
Photo Editor *Rose Deluhery*
Production Manager *Beth Kundert*
Production/Costing Manager *Sherry Padden*
Production/Imaging and Media Development Manager *Linda Meehan Avenarius*
Visuals/Design Freelance Specialist *Mary L. Christianson*
Marketing Manager *Pamela S. Cooper*
Copywriter *M. J. Kelly*

Basal Text *10/12 Times Roman*
Display Type *Helvetica*
Typesetting System *Macintosh™*
 QuarkXPress™
Paper Stock *70# Restorecote*

Brown & Benchmark
PUBLISHERS

Executive Vice President and General Manager *Bob McLaughlin*
Vice President of Production and New Media Development *Vickie Putman*
Vice President of Business Development *Russ Domeyer*
Director of Marketing *John Finn*

A Times Mirror Company

Sports and Fitness Series Consulting Editor: Aileen Lockhart, Texas Woman's University
Sports and Fitness Series Evaluation Materials Editor: Jane A. Mott, Texas Woman's University

Cover photograph © Michael Hart/FPG International

Proofread by Paula Gieseman

Library of Congress Catalog Card Number: 95–80431

ISBN 0–697–25627–8

Printed in the United States of America by Times Mirror Higher Education Group, Inc.,
2460 Kerper Boulevard, Dubuque, IA 52001

10   9   8   7   6   5   4   3   2   1

Contents

Basic Shots   41

3

Preface

In writing this book the authors have had two main objectives. The first objective is to provide the beginning racquetball player with an easy-to-follow sequence of playing techniques. The second objective is to instill an interest in a game that cannot only be played by the student while in school but has a carryover value into later life.

Before writing this new edition, the authors interviewed and discussed teaching techniques with many of the outstanding racquetball players in the country. These players included both the top male and female players. By doing this, it was hoped that a background of information could be compiled that would provide a foundation for the basic instructional procedures utilized in teaching the game of racquetball.

It is amazing how much racquetball has progressed in the past few years. It wasn't too long ago that racquetball players had a difficult time even finding a place to play, and little or no analysis of playing skills was available. The average players would find a court and then just bang away at the ball with little thought of either playing technique or game strategy. This textbook should fill the void for easy-to-understand instructions about the sport.

The material is organized in such a way that if a beginner follows the information in a step-by-step sequence, he or she will soon not only know the basic skills but also the strategy that will dictate the use of each particular skill. Each skill is accompanied by sequence photographs that illustrate critical movements of the various strokes. Practice drills are given so that a person can develop individual techniques without outside supervision or instruction. Care has been taken to make all of the instructions as simple as possible. It is the hope of the authors that individuals who utilize this book will soon become a part of the large group of current racquetball enthusiasts.

A section is included on the language of racquetball so that the learner will be able to communicate intelligently with other racquetball players.

The self-evaluative questions placed throughout the chapters are designed to help the reader combine specific information into a meaningful whole. The questions are not always positioned according to the presentation of given topics. This is done so that each individual will have to stop and think about what has been learned at a certain point, and in addition, the questions become guidelines to future reading. As students develop skill in racquetball, they should return to any questions that originally gave them trouble until they can answer them with ease.

The material in this text has been and is being used by hundreds of students in beginning racquetball classes in schools and racquetball clubs, and by individuals interested in learning the basic skills of racquetball.

The authors feel that racquetball is one of the most enjoyable games now being played and hope that the reader will soon agree.

Gratitude is extended to Nathan Passey, a member of Brigham Young University's nationally ranked racquetball team, who reviewed the manuscript and also served as the model for the photographs. Thanks is also given to Patrick J. Krohn who was responsible for the photography used in this edition.

RACQUETBALL

What Is Racquetball?

1

Welcome to the sport of racquetball. We are happy that you, like many other people, have decided to participate in this very enjoyable activity.

In this chapter, we will give you some information on how racquetball developed and then explain the basic procedures of the game. Next, we will provide information about the equipment, some safety rules to follow, and some ideas about conditioning, warm-up, and cool-down so that you will be better prepared to play the game.

Racquetball originated in the United States, developing out of the game of paddleball in the late 1940s. Earl Riskey of the University of Michigan is credited with being the individual who came up with the original concepts of the game. While watching tennis players practice their shots in a handball court, he decided that one could play a game that was similar to handball, but would also include the skills of tennis. It was necessary at first to use improvised equipment, for example, tennis balls and paddle tennis racquets. The first rules of the game came from handball, but as the game spread many local adaptations were added, especially in regard to the type of paddle racquet and ball utilized.

In 1949, Joe Sobek of Bridgeport, Connecticut, observed members of the Greenwich YMCA play a paddleball game in which a wooden paddle was used. He felt that the game could be improved by using a string racquet rather than a solid-faced wooden one, as the string racquet would afford better control and could impart better speed to the ball. The first ball was a pink rubber ball, similar to the inside of a tennis ball. Sobek also developed a softer blue ball that was used by many players.

As players from the Greenwich YMCA moved to other parts of the country, they introduced the new game and the sport increased in popularity. Sobek was instrumental in the spread of the game; he contributed equipment to various YMCAs so they could experiment with the new activity. As a result, the sport spread rapidly between 1949 and 1959.

In time the game was adopted by many YMCAs and recreation departments. Because of the inexpensive equipment and fast pace of the game, many people became interested in playing racquetball. Since one can get an excellent workout in approximately thirty minutes, many businessmen were attracted to the game. They found that much of their daily tension and frustration could be expended and released on the racquetball court. Also all ages and both sexes found the game easy to learn. During this time, and into the 1960s, the game spread and was played under many different names, such as "paddle-rackets," "paddle-ball," and "paddle tennis." On April 26, 1969, players and officials attended an organizational meeting in St. Louis and selected a name that was felt to describe the game well. It was

1

decided to officially adopt the name "racquetball" and the International Racquetball Association was formed. During this time, the first International Racquetball Association Championships were held. Today local, regional, and national championships are held for both men and women. The official organization for racquetball in this country is the American Amateur Racquetball Association (AARA), with headquarters in Colorado Springs, Colorado.

Since that time, the popularity of the game has spread, and one now finds players of all ages and both sexes playing racquetball. In order to become skilled in many activities, many hours of individual instruction and a great amount of practice time are required. The basic skills of racquetball, however, can be taught and learned in a relatively short period of time. The increase in interest, the development of facilities, and the addition of racquetball into physical education curricula have done much to promote the sport.

Racquetball is a fast game requiring endurance, skill, and body control. It requires the utilization of nearly all parts of the body. Because of its demands on the cardiorespiratory system, it ranks as an excellent conditioning activity. Research indicates that racquetball is an excellent means of providing the stimulus to bring about gains in endurance. Racquetball can help in the control of body weight because of the high caloric expenditure required in playing the game. In our sedentary society, there is a need for physical activity to relieve the stress and tension of modern life. The fact that racquetball provides a means of relieving this tension makes it worthwhile in the development of good mental health. Racquetball, however, needs no outside justification since it is a wonderful game to be enjoyed.

Racquetball is an excellent activity because it doesn't require a great amount of time to get a vigorous workout. In just thirty minutes, one can receive enough activity to gain many healthful benefits. It is played in many areas as an enjoyable corecreational activity; the pace of the game is adjusted to meet the skill level and ages of the competitors. Racquetball is one of those rare sports where you can obtain a tremendous conditioning stimulus, and also have fun and total enjoyment at the same time.

Racquetball may be played by two (singles), three (cutthroat), or four (doubles) players. It may be played on a one-, three-, or four-walled court. Most of the information in this book applies to four-walled courts, but the basic strokes and shots also apply to one- and three-walled courts.

Racquetball does not require a lot of expensive equipment and can be played anywhere a court is available. The rules of the game are simple and easy to learn and one can become quite proficient in the basic skills in a short time. Many people continue to play racquetball until they are quite old, utilizing strategy and experience to offset their lack of speed and endurance.

In addition to the fun of playing racquetball, what other attributes of the sport account for its popularity?

Endurance Training Guidelines

Increasing numbers of people are becoming involved in endurance training activities, and thus, there is a need for exercise prescription guidelines.

Based on the existing evidence concerning exercise prescribed for healthy people, the American College of Sports Medicine makes the following recommendations for the quantity and quality of training to develop and maintain cardiorespiratory fitness.

1. Frequency of training: 3–5 days per week.
2. Intensity of training: 60–90 percent of maximal heart rate.
3. Duration of training: 20–60 minutes of continuous aerobic activity. Duration is dependent on the intensity of the activity; therefore, lower intensity activity should be conducted over a longer period of time.
4. Mode of activity: any activity that uses large muscle groups, that can be maintained continuously, and is rhythmical and aerobic in nature.

A fairly valid and reliable indicator of intensity can be obtained by measuring the heart rate obtained during participation in activity. In order to determine the recommended heart rate necessary to achieve a training effect, you must know your maximal heart rate.

To determine your heart rate, you must be able to count your pulse. The pulse can be counted by placing the middle fingers over the carotid artery alongside the esophagus in the neck or over the radial artery on the thumb-side of the wrist.

It is possible to approximate your maximal heart rate by subtracting your age from 220. For example, a person twenty years of age would have an estimated maximal heart rate of two hundred beats per minute ($220 - 20 = 200$).

The heart rate necessary to bring about a training effect is in a zone that is between 60 and 90 percent of your maximal heart rate. To determine the heart rate you must achieve to ensure cardiovascular endurance training changes is a very simple matter. Take 60 percent of your maximal heart rate to find the lowest pulse you should have when training, and 90 percent of your maximal heart rate to determine an estimation of the highest pulse rate during an aerobic training workout.

Table 1.1 contains the average maximal heart rates and target zones for training effects for selected age groups.

It is important to count the pulse immediately upon stopping an exercise in order to determine the exercise heart rate, because it begins to decrease quite rapidly once the exercise is slowed or stopped. Find your pulse within five seconds and count the number of heartbeats for ten seconds; then multiply by six to determine your estimated exercise heart rate for one minute. Remember to start counting at zero.

Table 1.1   Average Maximal Heart Rates and Target Training Zones

Age	Maximal Heart Rate	60%	65%	70%	75%	80%	85%	90%
10	210	126	136	147	158	168	179	189
15	205	123	133	144	154	164	174	185
20	200	120	130	140	150	160	170	180
25	195	117	127	137	146	156	166	176
30	190	114	123	133	143	152	162	171
35	185	111	120	130	139	148	157	167
40	180	108	117	126	135	144	153	162
45	175	105	114	123	131	140	149	158
50	170	102	110	119	128	136	145	153
55	165	99	107	116	124	132	140	149
60	160	96	104	112	120	128	136	144
65	155	93	101	109	116	124	132	140
70	150	90	97	105	113	120	128	135
75	145	87	94	102	109	116	123	131
80	140	84	91	98	105	112	119	126
85	135	81	88	95	101	108	115	122

Procedure of the Game

To start the game, the server stands within the service zone and, after letting the ball bounce once, strikes it, causing it to rebound off the front wall. In order to be in play, the ball must then land behind the short line. The server is given two attempts on the serve. If the first serve is not legal, then he is given another serve. The opponent must then return the ball in such a manner that it will hit the front wall before it strikes the floor, and play continues until either the serving or receiving side is unable to return the ball legally. A point is won by the serving side if the receiver returns the ball illegally. If the server fails to return the ball, he or she loses the serve. The opponent now becomes the server and the former server now becomes the receiver. A complete game ends when one side receives fifteen points.

In doubles, each player is allowed to serve before a loss of team serve occurs, except in the case of the initial service of each game, when only one player serves. Either player on the doubles team may return the ball after it is in play.

A match consists of the first two out of three games.

The Racquetball Court

Figure 1.1 shows the measurements of four-, three-, and one-wall racquetball courts. The recommended four-wall court is 40 feet long and 20 feet wide, with a front wall of 20 feet and a back wall at least 12 feet high. The short line, parallel to the front wall, divides the playing court in half. The service line is parallel to and

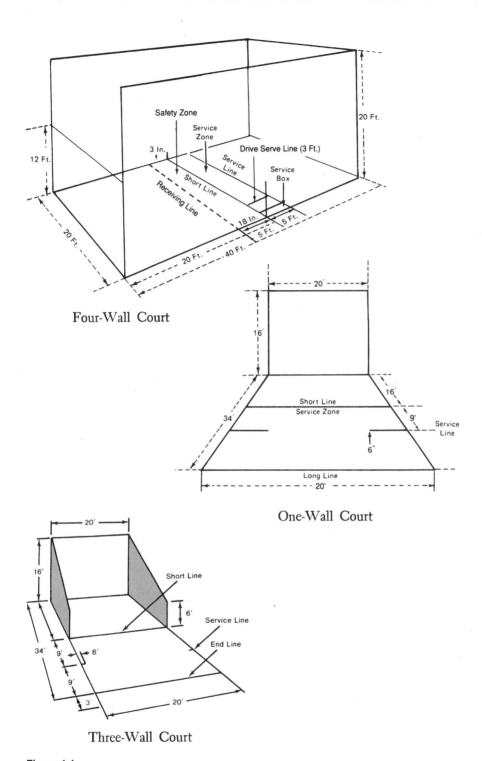

Four-Wall Court

One-Wall Court

Three-Wall Court

Figure 1.1
Racquetball courts

5 feet in front of the short line. The area between these two lines is designated as the service zone. A service box is located at each end of the service zone. It is marked with lines 18 inches from each sidewall and the line is parallel to the sidewall. Five feet behind the short line, broken lines are marked on the floor forming the receiving line. The receiver cannot attack the serve until the ball bounces past the short line or crosses the plane of the receiving line. The drive serve rule lines are three feet from each side wall in the service box, dividing the service zone into two seventeen-foot service zones for drive serves only. The safety zone is the five-foot area bounded by the back edges of the short line and the receiving line. This zone is observed only during the serve. Check the serving rules in Chapter 6 for further information concerning this zone. All lines are marked on the court with 1.5-inch red or white lines.

The one-wall court has a front wall that is 20 feet in width and 16 feet high. The floor is 20 feet wide and the length is 34 feet from the front wall to the back edge of the long line. There should be a minimum of 6 feet beyond the long line and each sideline in order to provide movement area for the players. The short line is 16 feet from the front wall. Parallel with the short line and 9 feet behind it are markers designating the service line. The imaginary extension and joining of these lines on the floor indicates the service zone. The receiving zone is the floor area behind the short line bounded by and including the long line and sidelines.

The three-wall dimensions are the same as the one-wall court, except that it has two sidewalls extending from the top of the front wall back along either sideline and slanting downward to a height of 6 feet at the short line, at which point they stop.

Equipment

Racquet

A short-handled racquet as shown in figure 1.2 must be utilized in racquetball. The racquet, including bumper guard and all solid parts of the handle, may not exceed 21 inches in length. Racquet strings may be gut, nylon, graphite, monofilament, plastic, metal, or a combination of these materials, providing the strings do not mark or deface the ball.

It is required that a thong be attached to the handle and slipped over the wrist of the player during the game. During play the hands may become wet with perspiration; this thong will prevent the racquet from slipping from the hand and striking another player.

Most racquets are either made of metal or a composite material, such as fiberglass or graphite. Composite racquets are an advantage because the strong fibers allow the racquet to have stiffness without adding extra weight. Longer fibers add to the stiffness of the racquet frame and this stiffness is sought by many elite players.

Two methods are utilized in the manufacturing of composite racquets. One method is termed injection molding and involves the placing of short fibers, such as

Figure 1.2
Racquets

fiberglass, into a mold. The second method is termed compression molding and uses longer fibers, such as graphite, which are placed in the mold by hand. Of the two types of molding, compression molding makes a better quality racquet. This is the type of racquet used by elite players in a hard-driving and fast-paced game. This type of racquet will also cost more.

Following are some advantages and disadvantages of various types of racquets.

Type of Racquet	Advantage	Disadvantage
Injection Molded	Inexpensive	Poor Balance, Quite Heavy, Too Flexible
Metal	Very Durable	Poor Balance, Heavy
Compression Molded	Good Control and Power	Expensive

The type of racquet you select will affect your style of play, so it is important to take time to look at many styles and types before making the final purchase. Pick the racquet up and swing it to test the grip, weight, and balance of the racquet. If possible, it would be helpful to rent a particular racquet that you might be interested in and take it into the court and hit some balls to determine how it feels and plays. Many professional stores offer "demo" racquets that can be used in determining the racquet that might be suited to your style of play.

Ball

Many different balls are manufactured by individual companies. The rules state that the ball should be 2.25 inches in diameter and should weigh approximately 1.40 ounces. When dropped from a height of 100 inches, the ball should bounce between 68 and 72 inches when the temperature is 70–74° F. Only a ball having the endorsement or approval of the AARA may be used in an AARA-sanctioned meet.

When purchasing a racquet, what are the important characteristics to consider, and how can you best determine whether a racquet is right for you?

Shoes and Socks

The comment that "the strength of an army lies in the feet of the soldier" is also true in racquetball. To avoid blisters and sore feet, you should make sure that you have good quality shoes that fit well. When purchasing a shoe, you should make sure that you are wearing the type of socks that you plan to wear while playing racquetball, not regular street socks. This will insure a proper fit for the racquetball shoes. The socks should be white and made of soft material, such as wool or cotton, and must be kept clean to prevent infections, such as athlete's foot. If a player is bothered by sore feet, friction can be reduced by rubbing the soles of the feet with petroleum jelly or a good commercial skin lubricant.

Uniform

According to the official racquetball rules, all parts of the uniform, consisting of shirt, shorts, and socks, shall be clean and white or of bright colors. Warm-up pants or shirts, if worn in actual match play, shall also be white or of bright colors. Only the club insignia, the name of the club, the name of the racquetball organization, the name of the tournament, or the name of the sponsor may be on the uniform. Players are not allowed to play without a shirt.

Accessory Equipment

In addition to the basic uniform of shoes, shorts, and shirts, many players utilize other accessory equipment, such as a glove, wristbands, and headbands. The purpose of the racquetball glove is to enable the player to obtain a firmer grip on the racquet during play. This is especially beneficial when moisture collects on the handle. By wearing wristbands and a headband, the player can eliminate much of the moisture that might otherwise interfere with match play.

Safety

Safety is an important factor in the game of racquetball. One of the key areas of the body to protect is the face, especially the eyes. Research indicates the ball may reach speeds of over 150 miles per hour and the racquet may be moving

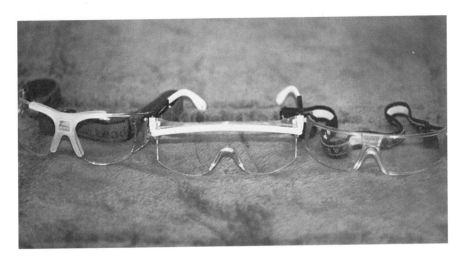

Figure 1.3
Some eyewear options currently available

as fast as 90 miles per hour on some strokes. To put this in perspective, a racquet-ball hit has the potential of carrying more energy than a .22 caliber bullet. Studies conducted at Pennsylvania State University revealed that open eye guard protective devices did not prevent balls fired at the head from hitting the eye on direct contact.

According to the racquetball rules, **eyewear designed for racquet sports is required apparel for all players.** Players who require corrective eyewear also must wear lensed eyewear designed for racquet sports.

Most eye guards have the lenses made of either polycarbonate or plastic. Plastic lenses are less impact resistant and scratch quite easily. Polycarbonate is the most impact resistant clear material that has been developed and has 7.6 times as much resistance as many plastic lenses. It weighs much less than plastic and can be coated to make it scratch resistant. Polycarbonate lenses are available with an antifog coating. Also it is possible to obtain polycarbonate lenses in a prescription range for individuals who normally wear regular glasses for visual corrections.

The American Amateur Racquetball Association recommends that players select eyewear with polycarbonate lenses with a three-millimeter center thickness. An updated list of approved eyewear can be obtained by writing the AARA at 1685 West Uintah, Colorado Springs, Colorado 80904–2921.

Figure 1.3 contains an example of some of the items that are currently on the market.

A few reminders will help you avoid being hit in the racquetball court.

1. Stay out of the path of the ball.
2. Protect your face.
3. Concentrate on what is taking place in the racquetball court so you can be aware where the ball will be when it is hit by either your opponent or partner.
4. Be aware of your opponent's position.

Warm-Up

Many minor aches and pains can be eliminated by engaging in a pregame warm-up routine. Warming up is a process that allows the body temperature to increase, and thus achieve better muscular efficiency. Some of the physiological factors that are thought to be responsible for this increased efficiency are: (1) the muscle contracts and relaxes faster as a result of increased temperatures; (2) the oxygen-carrying molecules, hemoglobin in the blood, and myoglobin in the muscle cell, release oxygen more readily as the body temperature increases; (3) the internal or viscous resistance inside the muscle is decreased, also the resistance to blood flow in the circulatory vessels is thought to be reduced; and (4) the metabolic activity of the cell mechanisms increase, which is thought to be a factor that could contribute to a better release of energy.

Electrocardiographic tracings of people engaging in strenuous activity without the use of a warm-up showed abnormal waves during the first minutes of exercise. These abnormal waves were absent when the exercise bout was preceded by a warm-up period of just two minutes.

A good way to start your warm-up period is through the use of stretching exercises. This will increase your flexibility and reduce the chance of muscle and joint injury. Racquetball is a game of mobility, quickness, and rapid change of direction. A few minutes of basic stretching exercises can contribute to being loose and ready to play. Most people tend to lack flexibility in the posterior thigh, anterior hip, low back, and chest—muscle groups that contribute much to the playing of racquetball.

Can you describe at least six safety procedures that should always be observed while playing racquetball?

The type of movement used in a stretching program is very important. Receptors located in the muscles and joints are stimulated by specific kinds of stretching movements. If you use fast, jerky, bouncy movements, this causes the muscle you are attempting to stretch to contract at the same time. This reduces the effectiveness of your stretching and often causes muscle soreness.

By using a slow, sustained stretch, the receptors cause the muscle to relax and lengthen, and thus aid in obtaining increased flexibility. Much of the muscle soreness is prevented or alleviated by this type of movement. When performing the stretching exercises, you should remember to **always use a slow, sustained stretch.**

In some cases you may find that some uncomfortable stiffness and soreness may develop in approximately twenty-four hours after you first start to play racquetball. This is due to the fact that you are probably starting to use muscles that haven't been involved in your daily activities. By engaging in a stretching program, you can get rid of much of this discomfort.

Figures 1.4–1.9 contain descriptions of some basic stretching exercises that are recommended for racquetball players.

Figure 1.4
Straight leg-bent knee stretch
Body Area: Lower Body
Starting Position: Sit upright on the floor and place the right foot against the inside of your left thigh so that a 90-degree angle is formed between the extended left leg and the flexed right leg.
Action: Keeping the left leg straight, lower the upper torso toward the thigh. Hold for 3–5 seconds and return to the starting position. Do this for 10 repetitions and then reverse the position of the legs.

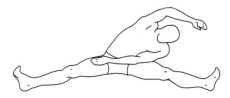

Figure 1.5
Straddle side stretch
Body Area: Lower Body and Midsection
Starting Position: Sit upright on the floor with the legs straight and as far apart as possible. Place the left arm toward the midsection of the body and raise the right arm overhead.
Action: Rotate the trunk and extend the upper torso toward the left leg. Hold for 3–5 seconds and return to the starting position. Do this for 10 repetitions and then reverse the position of the arms and stretch toward the right leg.

Figure 1.6
Prone quadriceps stretch
Body Area: Legs
Starting Position: Lie face down with the body extended and flex the right leg toward your buttocks.
Action: Grasp the ankle and pull the heel toward your buttocks. Make sure you do not place undue stress on the knee joint. Hold for 3–5 seconds and return to the starting position. Do this for 10 repetitions and then stretch the left leg.

Figure 1.7
Spinal twist
Body Area: Lower Body and Midsection
Starting Position: Sit upright on the floor with your left leg crossed over the right leg. Place the left arm behind you for support and place the right elbow on the outside of the left knee.
Action: Look over the left shoulder while turning the upper body and push back on the left knee with the right elbow. Hold for 3–5 seconds and return to the starting position. Do this for 10 repetitions and then reverse the position of the body.

Figure 1.8
Chair stretch
Body Area: Upper Body
Starting Position: While sitting or standing, flex the right arm toward the left shoulder and grasp the right elbow with the left hand.
Action: Pull the right elbow back toward the left shoulder. Hold for 3–5 seconds and return to the starting position. Do this for 10 repetitions and then reverse the position of the arms.

Figure 1.9
Towel stretch
Body Area: Upper Body
Starting Position: Stand upright with the right arm as far up the back as possible. Lift the left arm overhead while holding a towel and flex the elbow.
Action: Grasp the towel in both hands and pull the hands together. Hold for 3–5 seconds and return to the starting position. Do this for 10 repetitions and then reverse the position of the arms.

After you have completed your stretching, use the game of racquetball for the rest of your warm-up. You will not only warm up, but you will also be increasing your shot ability at the same time.

While you are warming up, think about the position of your body that is necessary in order to hit the ball in a proper manner. Mentally go through the correct movement sequence for each of your shots. Get the feel of the racquet and the feel of all of your shots. You can avoid many mistakes by using the pre-game time as a mental warm-up as well as a physiological warm-up.

The best indicator that the body is in a warmed condition is the onset of perspiration. The time you spend in warming up will be well worth the time and effort.

Cool-Down

A person should also be aware of the need for cooling down after a strenuous racquetball workout. Muscles sometimes tighten up and even go into painful spasms. This can be prevented or reduced by tapering off and allowing the body to return to a normal level of metabolic activity before going to the shower.

A series of one-way valves are located in the veins of the circulatory system in order to permit the flow of blood in only one direction. In order to assist the blood in circulating, you should taper off gradually by walking or jogging slowly for a few minutes. As the muscles contract during the cool-down period, they create pressure against the veins, which in turn aids in the return of blood to the heart. Without this cool-down period, the blood might pool in the lower body.

Cool down until you have stopped sweating profusely and your heart rate has dropped to 100 beats per minute or less.

How can you tell whether you have warmed up or cooled down sufficiently?

Essential Skills

2

Now that you have obtained the proper equipment and have a basic understanding of what the game of racquetball entails, you are ready to learn the essential skills of the game.

It is very important in learning to play racquetball to use good form. Good form will enable you to play a better game by increasing your power and directional control. Great personal satisfaction can be obtained from the game of racquetball if good form is utilized.

Control of the ball is lost if strokes are awkward, cramped, and jerky and if the racquet is constantly pushed in front of the body instead of making a free swing at one's side. Placing the wrong foot forward will throw the body off balance. A really good player will correct these faults.

You can avoid these common mistakes in swing and footwork if you will carefully follow the advice and recommendations given in this book. All of the instructions will be given for right-handed players.

Wrist Position (Fig. 2.1)

One of the important causes of error in racquetball is the improper position of the wrist when hitting the strokes. If you keep the wrist too stiff, the ball will be pushed rather than stroked toward the front, decreasing the amount of power you will be able to put on the ball.

One way to obtain the proper wrist position is to think of the action of a cobra as it is getting ready to strike. The wrist is held in a cocked back position at the start of the stroke and at the moment of contact is snapped or uncocked in order to impart maximum power on the ball. This is a coordinated movement that begins at the shoulder, moves to the wrist, and finally moves to the ball at impact. Figure 2.1 presents an example of this important concept.

Ready Position (Fig. 2.2)

In racquetball, the ready position is assumed prior to hitting any stroke. This position should be maintained while one faces the front wall until the ball is approaching the player. As the ball approaches, you can pivot toward the approaching ball and prepare to hit either a forehand or backhand shot. It is important that the weight be distributed on the balls of the feet while the ball is in play. At no time should the

Figure 2.1
Wrist position

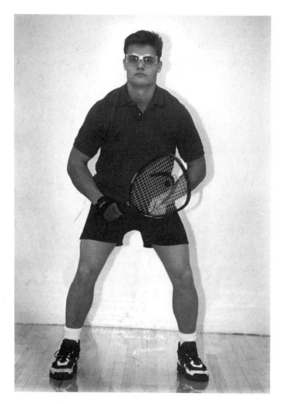

Figure 2.2
Ready position

player stand flat-footed. At all times the knees should be slightly bent so that playing position is low with the back kept straight. Many times players feel that they are getting low by bending the back rather than the knees.

The Forehand Stroke (Fig. 2.3)

The forehand stroke is fundamental in racquetball. This is the stroke that enables you to keep the ball in play. It allows you to get into the proper position after the ball has been hit and eventually enables you to position yourself to put the ball away, or to get the ball past the opponent.

The forehand stroke is a very natural one. With your body turned to face the sidewall, draw the racquet back until it points towards the back wall, then draw the racquet forward to meet the ball knee-high.

Grip

To be able to swing the racquet back and then forward to meet the ball, you need to know how to hold the racquet properly. The grip that is recommended is known as the handshake grip.

Stand the edge of the frame of the racquet on a table or on the floor with the handle pointing towards the body. Now, shake hands with the handle so that the V formed by the thumb and index finger is directly on top of the racquet handle. The thumb and fingers will overlap the handle so that both the thumb and fingers will close around the handle in a comfortable manner. You should have the index finger extended slightly, and the heel of the palm should touch the very end of the racquet, parallel with the end of the racquet but not overlapping. The palm of the hand will now be in the same plane as the face of the racquet.

Backswing

In order to execute a good forehand drive in tennis, a long swing is necessary to generate more speed. In racquetball, however, this swing must be shortened in order to move the racquet fast enough to make contact with the ball (due to the smaller court area). You can still generate good speed and power when shortening the swing if you remember to use the proper wrist action. As the ball approaches, the racquet is drawn back around head height or slightly higher and the wrist is fully cocked. A very important thing to remember is to keep the elbow of the hitting arm elevated as this aids in the generation of power in the ensuing stroke. The left arm is slightly in front of the body and the knees are slightly bent with the back in a fairly straight position. The body is turned so that your nonhitting shoulder is now facing the front wall.

Forward Swing

As the racquet is swung forward, the body weight is shifted from the right foot to the left foot. This is accomplished by stepping out with the left leg about 13 to 20 inches as you transfer the weight to the front foot. As you stride into the ball, you should dip the hitting shoulder to help lower the racquet. As you swing into the

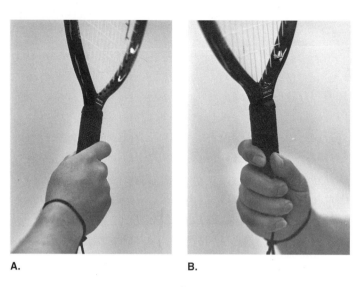

A. **B.**

C. **D.**

Figure 2.3
The forehand stroke. (A and B) The proper grip, (C) the backswing, (D and E) the forward swing, (F) impact, (G and H) follow-through.

ball, the right knee bends and the left arm starts to pull the body through the stroke. As the forward swing continues, the wrist remains in a cocked position with the racquet pointing backwards. The right arm is bent at the elbow and tucked in close to the side of the body. The body is now in a position to generate tremendous power at the time of impact.

Impact

The most important movement in the forward swing is when the racquet meets the ball. Contact is made with the ball from off the front foot. Just before you make

E.   F.

G.   H.

Figure 2.3
Continued

impact, you should snap the wrist forward so that the racquet face is vertical and traveling in a straight line into the ball. If you have enough time, you should let the ball drop as low as you can before hitting it. This will allow you to keep it low on the front wall. You can accomplish a low hitting position by bending the knees, dropping the hitting shoulder, and pivoting the hips into the shot. It is also important to emphasize the need to maintain visual contact with the ball during the stroke in order to assure a proper stroke. This helps you to keep the head down through impact and ensures a powerful and accurate shot.

Follow-Through

As the wrist is snapped through the ball, the left arm moves out of the way to pull the body through the final part of the stroke. The body remains low, with bent legs, until the stroke is completed. The racquet continues up behind the left side of the head. It is important that you maintain good balance at the end of the stroke so that you can quickly move in any direction in order to be ready to play your opponent's return shot.

The Backhand Stroke (Fig. 2.4)

In order to become a proficient racquetball player, you must have a good backhand stroke. At first this stroke may feel uncomfortable, but by utilizing the proper techniques and body position, you can, with practice, learn a backhand stroke that will be both accurate and powerful.

Grip

If you have enough time, it is best to switch the grip from the forehand grip to a backhand grip. This is accomplished by moving the hand to the left on the handle until the V formed by the thumb and index finger is directly on top of the left diagonal of the racquet handle. See figure 2.4 for an indication of the proper position for the backhand. This grip allows for a better range of motion in the wrist and also a better placement of the thumb that applies the necessary pressure for a good backhand stroke. By practicing this change, you will find that it will be possible to switch grips quite rapidly. If you have enough time, you can use the nonhitting hand to assist you in changing grips. Make sure, though, that this will not interfere with your swing and slow you down.

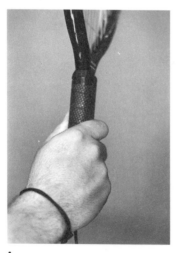

A.   B.

Figure 2.4
The backhand stroke. (A) The proper grip, (B) the correct stance and back swing, (C and D) the forward swing, (E) impact, (F and G) follow-through.

C.

D.

E.

F.

G.

Figure 2.4
Continued

Sometimes in the course of playing, especially when you hit shots in the front court or on the fly before the ball bounces, you will not have time to switch from a forehand grip. In this case, you want to make sure that the racquet face is in a vertical plane at the time of impact with the ball. This type of grip will cut down on the power of your backhand, so try to hit as accurate a shot as possible.

Stance

The stance for the backhand drive is the exact opposite of that for the forehand drive. As the ball approaches a player's backhand, the body pivots to the left facing the left sidewall. This is accomplished by stepping forward toward the ball, with the right foot pointing diagonally toward the left sidewall. Body position should be such that the right shoulder points toward the front wall and the left shoulder points toward the back wall. The right foot will be toward the front wall and ahead of the left foot. The feet should run in a parallel line to the left sideline. As you step forward with the right foot, weight should also be forward on this foot with the knees slightly bent, putting the weight on the balls of the feet.

Backswing

In setting up for the shot, it is important to get the racquet back as quickly as possible. This will keep you from using a short, punching type of stroke. As the racquet is pulled back, the wrist is fully cocked. One way to check to see if the wrist is cocked is to make sure the racquet head is up and in line with the forearm. This puts the racquet in the proper position for a powerful stroke. The hitting arm is bent at the elbow and the knees are in a bent position, with the shoulders rotated, so that the racquet is approximately head high. An important key is to have the plane of the chest almost parallel with the back wall. The body is now in position for the forward swing.

Forward Swing and Impact

At the completion of the backswing, it is necessary to start swinging the racquet forward toward the ball. You do this by stepping forward and shifting the weight to the front leg. As you do this, the hitting arm starts to extend, but the racquet is still back with the wrist in a cocked position. This is accomplished by rotating the shoulders and pivoting the hips into the shot. Just before you make contact with the ball, the hitting arm is nearly extended and the wrist is starting to snap as the shoulder pulls the racquet through the stroke. Contact with the ball is made in front of the foot, and at the moment of impact the hitting arm is fully extended and the wrist snaps through the ball. The elbow of the hitting arm is about 6 to 10 inches from the body at the moment of impact. It is important to keep your eyes on the ball at all times in order to maintain a proper body position. Even though the wrist snaps through the ball, the racquet should be vertical at impact and shouldn't roll over as you hit the ball. This will help to maintain accuracy along with the power.

Follow-Through

As contact with the ball is made, the racquet should follow through to the right side of the body. In the beginning of the follow-through, the wrist is held firm and the racquet is still vertical to give maximum direction to the shot. The legs remain bent in order to keep the body low. The hitting shoulder is pulled through and the racquet continues on a horizontal plane at about waist height for a complete follow-through. Always maintain good body balance so that you are ready to move to a position for a return shot.

The Continental Grip

We believe that all beginners should start using the handshake grip that has been described previously in this chapter. This grip allows the beginner to completely close all the fingers with the thumb locked on the first finger, which we feel will give the player a tighter grip as well as good control of the racquet. However, as players advance in their skill, technique, and experience in racquetball, they may want to vary that grip somewhat. Another grip with slight variation from the handshake grip is the continental grip. The one advantage of this grip over the handshake grip is that it allows a player to hit the forehand and backhand with basically the same grip and with very little change or adjustment. Therefore, it will reduce the problems of changing grips whenever the player is forced to hit the ball quickly and in changing from one stroke to another during a rally.

Forehand (Fig. 2.5)

To assume the forehand grip, use the same procedure as explained previously in assuming the grip as explained on page 17, the only difference being that the index finger, or the first finger, is now squarely against the back of the handle rather than curling around into a locked position with the thumb, as explained in the handshake grip. What this allows is more finger spread on the grip, as opposed to the total closed finger position that is required for the handshake grip. Therefore, this would possibly give better control, inasmuch as you have more range of motion covered on the racquet handle.

You will note in looking down at your grip now that a V has been formed by the thumb and first finger on top of the racquet handle or slightly to the left edge of the grip. Please note that the thumb is now curled over the handle to lock against the second finger, as the first finger, or index finger, is now against the back of the handle grip. The angle formed by the arm and the racquet is very important in the use of this stroke. The following diagrams illustrate the improper and proper angle to be utilized.

The other mechanics of the continental forehand stroke, such as stance, backswing, forward swing, impact, and follow-through, are exactly the same as explained and illustrated in the handshake forehand discussion.

A.

B.

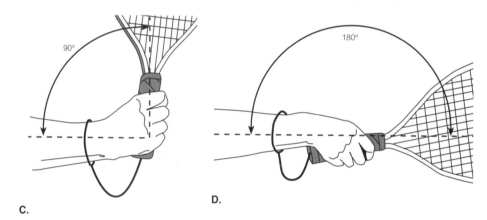

C.

D.

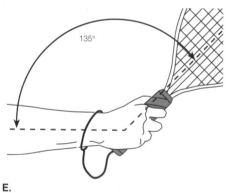

E.

Figure 2.5

The continental grip: forehand. (A) The thumb curls over the handle to lock against the
second finger. (B) A **V** is formed by the thumb and the first finger. (C) The angle formed by
the arm and the racquet is not enough of an angle. (D) The angle formed by the arm and the
racquet is too much of an angle. (E) The proper angle.

A.

B.

Figure 2.6
The continental grip: backhand. (A) The thumb stretches diagonally along the backside of the racquet handle. (B) A V should form on the top part of the handle when the racquet is held perpendicular to the floor.

Backhand (Fig. 2.6)

The same grip used for the forehand can also be used for the backhand with very little adjustment. The proper placement of the grip is illustrated in figure 2.6. In looking down at your racquet and grip, you should see a V formed on the top part of the handle when the racquet is held perpendicular to the floor. The V should be to the left of the center of the grip. The fingers must be held tightly together to maintain both good control and power. This grip may be assumed by slightly shifting or turning the hand to the left so that all the fingers now come together and so that the thumb is spread diagonally on the backside of the racquet handle. This grip differs from the handshake backhand grip in that the knuckles on the hand do not point upwards toward the ceiling as much and the thumb stretches diagonally along the backside of the grip rather than parallel to it. The value of this grip over the handshake grip is that the adjustment can be made more quickly.

Can you take the correct forehand grip, hit the ball to the front wall, and then change to the backhand grip to make a successful return? Using forehand strokes, can you stroke the ball continually to the front wall 6 times without missing? 12 times? 20 times? Can you do the same number of hits alternating forehand and backhand strokes?

Again, the mechanics of the continental backhand stroke, such as stance, backswing, forward swing, impact, and follow-through, are the same as the handshake backhand.

Regardless of what grip you use, the important thing is to have total control of the racquet and to feel comfortable with the grip.

The Importance of Keeping One's Eyes on the Ball

In most sports, keeping one's eyes on the ball at all times when the ball is in play is a vital and important factor. Such is also the case in racquetball. You must keep your eyes on the ball or watch the ball into the center of the racquet in order to hit it at exactly the right moment in order to generate speed and, most importantly, placement and direction. It is vital to look at the ball even to the point of looking at the spot where the ball was after the racquet has made contact and has hit the ball on its flight forward. The follow-through of the swing pulls the body and eyes around so that the body is now facing the front wall and can pick up the direction of the ball from this follow-through motion. If a player cheats by taking the eyes off the ball a split second before making contact with it, he or she will not be able to execute a good shot with adequate speed or proper direction.

The racquet should be examined after it has been used a number of times to see that the strings are getting the most use in the center of the racquet. If this is the case, then the ball is surely being hit in the proper place. The important key to playing a successful racquetball game is in watching the ball, not the opponent or any part of one's own body or swing. The eyes should constantly be kept on the ball throughout the playing of a match. This will allow for a determination of the ball's speed and bounce and the way it must be played on a return.

It is a common fault of most beginners to turn both their head and body toward the back wall after they have stroked the ball to see where it has landed and to watch their opponent return the ball to the front wall. In doing this, you put yourself out of position to be ready for the next shot; you also take the chance of being hit in the face by the returned ball. You also face the chance of getting beat by the returning ball by being out of position and having to make a complete turn to the front wall.

Which is most important and why: to watch the ball, the opponent, or your racquet arm as you prepare for, execute, and follow through a stroke?

In order for the shot to be good, the ball must return to the front wall; therefore, this turn toward the back wall is totally wasted and could cost you either a point or a sideout.

The Serve

The serve is very important in the game of racquetball, as every point begins with the serve and the serve is the only time you get to hold the ball and place it where you want in order to hit the ball.

This is the only stroke in the game that enables a player to take enough time to observe the position of the opponent and to get ready for the return stroke. Thus, this time is a definite advantage.

The serve should be used by beginners with the same philosophy used in learning the forehand and backhand strokes: accuracy is developed before speed. One of the most common mistakes of the beginning player is to try to hit the ball too hard. One must realize that competent players who hit the ball with ease and speed have probably played the game for many years and consequently they make it look easy because of the experience they have had on the court. However, all of these players started by placing the ball accurately before applying complete speed to their drives, smashes, and serves. Speed must be increased gradually only after the point where the ball is consistently hit to the frontcourt and placed on the frontcourt as desired. If a beginner tries to hit the ball too hard, improvement will be delayed and skill will come much slower.

The serve in its simplest form merely puts the ball in play, but a strong, well-placed serve gives you a fine opportunity to get an advantage on your opponent; you can and should make full use of this advantage.

There are four basic serves in racquetball—the drive serve, the garbage serve, the lob serve, and the Z-serve. The most used serve is the drive serve. This is the serve that will be most used when a beginner develops playing skills and becomes proficient in the game. However, even with the best players and the best servers, there is a time in everyone's game when the drive serve may not be landing as it should. It may be off just a degree so that the opponent is returning it to the front wall with ease. It is at this time that you might feel the need to change to a different serve in order to make the game competitive. Two serves that can be very effective are the lob serve and the garbage serve. These serves can be used without excessive power or strength and can give a player a period of recovery or rest during the match if the player tires at any time. The Z-serve is a more difficult serve to master, but it has the advantage of hitting a multiple of walls, and if your opponent is confused by the way the ball rebounds off the wall, it can be very effective.

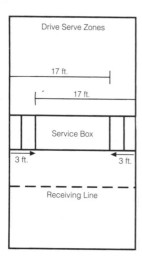

Figure 2.7
The drive service zone

One important point to remember when serving is to stand in approximately the center of the serving area. If you stand too close to either sidewall, you will be giving up the most important center court position. Also you won't be able to serve the ball to either side of the court.

Serve the majority of the time to the opponent's weakness, which in most instances is the backhand. This will limit the opponent's ability to hit a strong return and will allow you to control the game.

In serving, you must allow the ball to bounce once before hitting it, and the ball must then strike the front wall before making contact with the sidewalls. The ball must pass the short line on the fly to be good and if you hit three walls, including the front wall, on the fly, the serve is a fault. Any serve that hits either the ceiling or the back wall after hitting the front wall is also a fault. Two consecutive faults result in a loss of serve, and any serve that hits a wall before contacting the front wall is an out.

Any serve that hits the crotch of the front wall and floor, the crotch of the front wall and sidewall, or the crotch of the front wall and ceiling is known as a crotch serve and is an out serve because it did not hit the front wall first. Any serve that rebounds into the crotch of the back wall and the floor or hits the crotch of the sidewall and floor, beyond the short line, is a legal serve and must be played.

Why is it important to stand in approximately the center of the serving zone as you serve the ball?

The Drive Serve (Fig. 2.8)

The serve that determines a consistent winner is the drive serve. Weak serves either result in long rallies or give your opponent an opportunity to take the offensive. The drive serve produces aces, or your opponent may hit a weak return and thus give you an excellent chance to win the point.

The drive serve is controlled by a specific racquetball rule. Figure 2.7 shows the drive service zone.

The drive serve rule lines are three feet from each sidewall in the service box and this divides the service area into two seventeen-foot service zones for drive serves only.

The player may drive serve to the same side of the court in which the server is standing as long as the start and finish of the service motion takes place outside the three-foot line.

The service stroke should be delivered with a free, rhythmic swing in a continuous motion. A complete range of motion can be utilized on the serve, whereas in the forehand and backhand strokes the speed of the ball will sometimes dictate the use of a short rather than a full swing. The service should be smooth, uncramped, and without a hitch. In order to get power in a serve, your body weight must be put behind the ball by shifting the body weight forward. By using a proper backswing and forward swing, the racquet has time to pick up speed and should be traveling at its fastest speed when it contacts the ball (fig. 2.8).

Stance

To begin the serve, the body is turned to the right so that it is facing the right wall. The left shoulder should be in line with the front wall and the right shoulder in line with the back wall. The right leg is slightly bent and the left leg bent a little more than the right leg. The arms are fully extended and the ball is held near the racquet. During this time, look at the ball and visualize mentally how you plan to hit the ball.

In order to disguise your serve, start all of your serves in the same manner. Otherwise, your opponent will be able to anticipate the serve and adjust quickly in order to hit a better return.

Grip

The grip for the serve is the same as that used for the forehand stroke. The most used grip is the handshake grip, as described previously. As contact is made with the ball on the serve, the hand should grip the racquet handle tightly. It is said that a good player squeezes a little "sawdust" out of the end of the racquet as contact is made with the ball.

Dropping the Ball

Once the service stance has been assumed facing the right sidewall with knees slightly bent, the left arm and hand are extended, holding the ball immediately in front of the body and toward the right sideline, in a straight line opposite the chest or slightly below. Now the ball can be dropped to the floor from this position just as though it was a rock or an egg dropping from the hand. The ball will have sufficient bounce to hit it, so it is not necessary to throw the ball; rather, it drops from the hand position. As the ball hits the floor and bounces upward, the backswing must be coordinated with the shifting of weight from the left foot to the back foot (right foot).

Figure 2.8
The drive serve. (A) Dropping the ball, (B) the backswing, (C) the forward swing, (D) impact, (E) follow-through.

Backswing

As has been previously mentioned, a full swing is necessary in order to generate speed and power. The farther back the racquet is drawn, the longer the forward swing will be and the faster the racquet will be moving when it hits the ball. As the ball comes up from the floor, the racquet is drawn back as far as can be comfortably done with the elbow bent. As the racquet is drawn back, weight is shifted from the left foot to the right foot. This is the position in which to make a forward swing. Notice how the racquet is cocked in order to generate power with the wrist at impact. Here especially, the critical point is the elevation of the right elbow. At the peak of the backswing, the elbow should be at least at the height of the shoulder.

Forward Swing and Impact

As the racquet is swung forward, the weight is shifted from the right foot to the left foot as you stride into the ball. At the moment of impact, the left leg extends forward and the right knee is bent, in order for the hitting shoulder to drop as you pivot into the ball with your right hip.

The timing of the drive serve should be such that the ball is hit below knee level. As the ball nears the floor, the hitting wrist drops low and the arm straightens out with a full wrist snap through the ball. On the forward swing, the elbow must come down before the wrist. This causes a "whip" effect and generates the greatest amount of power.

You should aim for a spot on the front wall about three feet up and one foot to the left of the center of the front wall to serve to the backhand and three feet up and one foot to the right of the center of the front wall to serve to the forehand.

Follow-Through

The follow-through is important. After the racquet has hit the ball, it should follow through forward and then to the left of the body. No attempt should be made to stop the forward swing of the racquet or the forward motion of the body after the ball has left the racquet. The follow-through of the swing should pull the body forward and around so that it is now in good playing position to receive the ball as it is hit back to the front wall by the opponent.

Drive Serve Variations: Backhand and Forehand (Fig. 2.9)

These two variations of the drive serve are the most common and effective of all the serves in racquetball. The ball is hit hard to the front wall and slightly off the center. It should travel fast toward the rear corner and be low enough to rebound off the floor. The ball should be hit low enough to prevent any rebound from the back wall. This forces an opponent to return the ball after the rebound. Even if the ball is hit high, but close to the sidewall, the rebound will be such that an opponent will be forced to swing from a crowded or bent-arm position. At all times one should attempt to achieve good serve placement and direction, in order to inhibit an opponent's swing.

Another variation is to hit the ball low, just beyond the short line so that it rebounds a second time just before the back wall.

The Garbage Serve (Fig. 2.10)

Earlier in the chapter, the necessity and advantage of having more than one serve was mentioned. The drive serve is used the most, but a player needs other serves to combine with the drive serve. Such a serve is the garbage serve. It can be very effective in different situations and at certain times during a match. The garbage serve is hit in the air above your opponent's head. It should be placed as high and as close to the wall and back corner as possible, so that the opponent has difficulty making a full swing at the ball when returning it to the front wall.

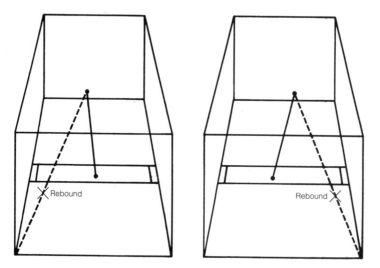

Figure 2.9
Drive serve variations

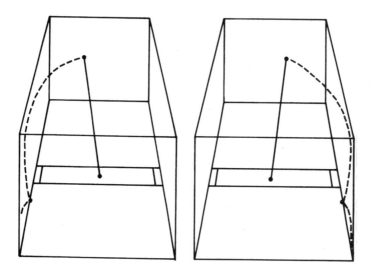

Figure 2.10
Garbage serves

The stroke is a push rather than the hard and powerful stroke used in the drive serve.

Stance

Assume the same type of stance as in the drive serve.

Dropping the Ball

In dropping the ball, allow the ball to rebound so that it peaks at about chest height.

Backswing

As you bring the racquet back, use a backswing similar to that in the drive serve, except the body is more erect and the knees are not bent as much, as you will be hitting the ball at a higher arc in the garbage serve.

Forward Swing and Impact

As the racquet is swung forward, the weight is shifted from the right foot to the left foot, the knees are slightly bent, and the body leans forward toward the ball. Notice that the body is still more erect than in the drive serve. This allows you to make contact with the ball at a higher arc. You must not get too close to the ball as this cramps your swing. Also a much slower swing is utilized in this serve.

When contact is made at a point between the waist and the chest, the stroke is a push toward the front wall. Allow the racquet face to tilt backward as you make contact with the ball, and this will cause the ball to travel in an upward direction. Aim for a spot midway up the front wall and approximately one foot to either the left or right of the center of the front wall. The ball should now rebound about 5 feet behind the short line and then bounce upward and drop into the back corner.

Follow-Through

As the racquet makes contact with the ball, the body should be moving forward toward the ball and the weight should be shifting to the left foot. After the racquet has hit the ball, it should follow through forward and upward so that the racquet is now immediately overhead in a straight line and slightly to the left. If you wish the serve to be shorter and not as high in nature, then it is necessary to check the forward swing before it gets to its final position. Follow-through is not as important as it is in the drive serve, as the body is already facing the front wall and you are in good position to recover and receive the ball as it is hit back to the front wall by your opponent.

Garbage Serve Variations: Backhand and Forehand

The ball is hit high on the front wall slightly off the center and in such a manner that it makes a high bounce to the rear corner of the court. The force on the ball should cause the ball to just reach the back wall after rebounding from the floor. From this rebound the ball should then drop down, making it an extremely difficult serve to return.

By effectively placing the ball with a high bounce close to the sidewall, your opponent will have a difficult time in making a full swing.

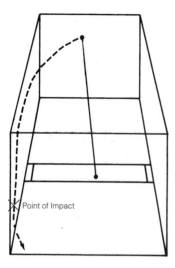

Figure 2.11
Lob serve

Lob Serve (Fig. 2.11)

The lob serve is a higher version of the garbage serve and utilizes the sidewall on the downward trajectory. The serve is hit exactly like the garbage serve, except that you aim at a spot about three-fourths of the way up on the front wall and more than a foot to the left or right of the center of the front wall. This will determine whether the serve will go to either the forehand or the backhand and will cause the ball to hit the sidewall before hitting the floor. As the ball rebounds from the front wall, it should strike the sidewall no more than 6 feet up from the floor and about 6 feet in front of the back wall. By making contact with the sidewall, you will be able to keep the ball from rebounding hard off the back wall and giving your opponent an easy shot.

Since it is important that the ball hit the sidewall as it descends, the lob serve is usually a more difficult serve to control than the garbage serve. Also, since you serve the ball with a higher elevation, the ball is in the air longer and your opponent may anticipate the serve and hit it on the fly for a strong offensive return.

Z-Serve

The Z-serve gets its name from the pattern the ball traverses during the flight from the front wall to the rear corner of the court. It is an especially effective serve against players who have a hard time following the flight of the ball and who do not read the rebound of the ball off the wall very well. The Z-serve can be hit to either the backhand or the forehand. The Z-serve can be used either as a low Z-serve

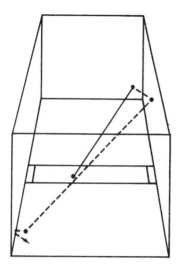 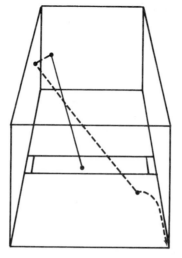

Figure 2.12
Low Z-serve

Figure 2.13
High Z-serve

or a high Z-serve. In Z-serves, you take a serving position a few feet from the center of the service zone to keep from being in the path of the served ball.

Low Z-Serve (Fig. 2.12)

The low Z-serve is hit the same way as the drive serve. The most effective low Z-serve is one that is hit to the backhand. Aim for a spot on the front wall about 3 to 4 feet up on the front wall and about 1 foot in from the right sidewall. After hitting the front wall, the ball should travel into the right sidewall and then travel across the playing court into the left rear corner, where it strikes the floor and then rebounds about 4 feet up from the floor and 4 feet from the back wall.

If the ball is served properly, the amount of spin placed on the ball will cause it to come off the left sidewall parallel to the back wall. This is a very difficult shot to return and leaves the person returning the shot in poor court position.

High Z-Serve (Fig. 2.13)

The high Z-serve is a change-of-pace serve, and the stroke for this serve is more like the push stroke used in the garbage serve. The ball is served with about 50 percent power to a spot about 12 to 15 feet up on the front wall and 1 foot from the sidewall. It will then rebound into the sidewall and travel with a high arching motion toward the rear corner and strike the floor, then hit the sidewall with little speed, and drop in the corner near the back wall.

The benefit of the high Z-serve is that if your opponent does not hit the serve before it bounces on the floor, it will die against the back wall. This serve can be hit to your opponent's forehand quite effectively.

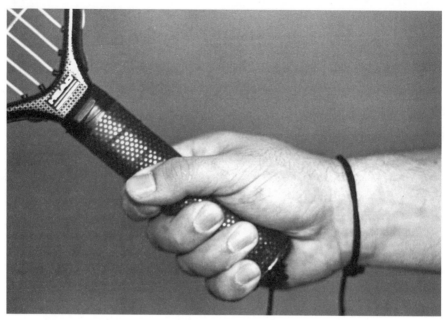

A.

B.   **C.**

Figure 2.14
The overhead smash. (A) The grip, (B) the stance, (C) the back swing, (D) the upward swing, (E) the forward swing and impact, (F) follow-through.

Overhead Smash (Fig. 2.14)

The overhead smash in racquetball is made with practically the same swing as that used in the serve in tennis. However, as there is no net to contend with in racquetball and since the ball can land practically three feet closer to the floor, it is not necessary to put a slice or cut on the ball.

D.

E.

F.

Figure 2.14
Continued

In racquetball the ball is hit with a flat racquet face, as opposed to cutting or slicing the ball. The smash is utilized when the ball comes off the front wall to the player in such a manner that it is high and above the head.

Beginners should not worry about developing the overhead smash until all other phases of the game have been developed. Every ball, regardless of how high it might be in coming, will always drop down to a position where the forehand or backhand drive can be used.

It is not necessary to have a smash in order to be a good racquetball player, but if a person has had some experience with it, there are certain times and instances where it can improve the overall game.

This stroke should be executed with the same type of motion as the forehand, backhand, and drive serve strokes. It should be a continuous motion, a rhythmic swing without pause. Since the stroke utilizes a backswing, an upward swing, a forward swing, and a follow-through, one must remember that, in order for it to be effective, the stroke must be used with a long, free swing.

How do the low Z- and high Z-serves differ from each other, and why are the Z-serves difficult to return?

Grip

The grip for the overhead smash is primarily the same as the handshake forehand grip. A good player can utilize this grip and be very effective with the overhead smash. However, if the oncoming ball does allow enough time to make a slight shift in grip, it is desirable to use a grip that falls somewhere between the handshake forehand grip and the backhand grip. This is accomplished by:

1. Shaking hands with the handle of the racquet as is done in the forehand grip.
2. Shifting the palm one-eighth of a turn to the left instead of the one-fourth turn for the backhand grip.
3. The hand should be at the end of the racquet handle and wrapped around the handle so that the thumb touches the first finger.

Stance

The stance for the overhead smash is a diagonal stance toward the front wall. The left foot should point diagonally toward the front wall and the right foot should be somewhat pointed toward the right wall. Weight should be evenly distributed on both feet and as the backward swing is started, weight should shift to the right foot. Then, as the upward swing is begun, the weight should be on the right foot. In taking the proper position for the smash, the left shoulder should be pointing toward the front wall and the right shoulder toward the back wall.

Backswing

As the right arm is drawn down, the racquet is pulled away from the left hand, which has been acting as a balancer for control. The racquet should be pulled straight down, close to the body and to the right foot. As the racquet is drawn down, body weight is shifted from the left foot back to the right foot. The backward swing continues until the arm is fully extended and is as far back as it can comfortably be drawn.

Upward Swing

Now the racquet is ready to be drawn upward, and as this is done the elbow is bent in order to impart speed and power to the swing. Also, bending the elbow will help to hit the ball high in the air and directly over the right eye, the ideal place to make contact with the ball. If the elbow is not bent, the shot will lack the power a player is trying to achieve. Bending the elbow also increases the accuracy of the shot.

After bending the elbow, the racquet is carried upward until the handle is to the right of the ear. This will put the racquet in position to begin the forward swing.

Forward Swing

As the racquet starts forward, the elbow is gradually straightened out, as it is desirable to hit the ball directly over the right eye with the arm fully extended and the ball as high in the air as can be reached with this full extension. As the racquet swings forward, weight is shifted from the right foot forward to the left foot. This will enable the body to move forward with the complete swing. You should remember at all times to coordinate the backward, upward, and forward swing in one smooth motion without any pause.

Impact

The ball can be hit effectively with a flat racquet face, without cutting across the ball. By hitting it with the flat racquet face, much speed and power can be generated. The main thing to remember in meeting the ball is that contact be made when the ball is high above the right eye with the arm fully extended. Coordination of the entire swing, so that the ball is met at the proper time, is the key to making the smash successful.

One common fault of novice players is to pull back as they make contact with the ball. Can you explain why this reduces power and may affect the direction of the hit?

Follow-Through

After contact has been made with the ball, the racquet is allowed to follow through forward toward the front wall and down across the body to the left side. The momentum of the racquet follow-through should completely pull the right foot up and forward, so that the body is now facing the front wall and in position for the opponent's return of the ball.

Once you have mastered the essential skills, you are ready to utilize them in perfecting all of the shots in racquetball.

Helpful Hints for the Beginner

Even a beginning racquetball player can usually stand back and make a logical assessment of mistakes—what went wrong during that part of a game where a mistake was made. It is a fairly easy game in which to analyze what you are doing wrong and to determine how to correct the things that need correcting. When play is not going as it should, there are some essential skills you can check for proper execution and some basic points to remember. Some of these are:

1. *Concentration.* You must have total concentration, especially in relationship to the ball, if your game is to be effective. By this we mean the player should be sure to watch the ball into the racquet and to keep the head down in relationship to the ball, as one would in hitting a golf ball, rather than peeking up just at the moment the ball makes contact. This is a mistake that will result in not hitting the ball squarely with the power that would otherwise be gained if the eyes had been kept on the ball for that extra split second. Concentration on this skill contributes greatly to the success of a racquetball player.

2. *Grip.* In order to get power, direction, and placement on the ball, a player must have a tight, controlled grip on the racquet at the moment contact is made with the ball. Many beginning players hit the ball with a loose and wobbly racquet, therefore lacking the proper speed and power or direction and placement that they should have in making their different shots. It is imperative for a player to have total control of the racquet through a proper grip in order to execute the desired shot.

3. *Hitting through the ball.* It is a common tendency for beginning players, as they make contact with the ball, to pull back and away from their swing rather than continuing through the swing. Pulling back results in a loss of power and speed and probably inaccurate direction and placement. Hitting through the ball is a simple fundamental that requires concentration; stay with the swing in relationship to the ball in order to make the shot effective.

4. *Anticipation.* After completing the swing and follow-through on the ball, the player must move the feet in anticipation of where the opponent is going to return the ball. The player is then in the best possible position to hit the ball again. Racquetball is a game that requires movement and at no time does it allow a player to stand; rather, the player must hit and move constantly in anticipation of where the ball is going to be returned.

The player who will go back and review these basic fundamentals and skills and try to keep these things in mind during play will find that proficiency and skill will improve immensely. These people will become better players faster and will enjoy the game of racquetball to a greater extent.

Basic Shots

3

All of the basic shots in racquetball can be executed by using the forehand stroke, the backhand stroke, and, in some cases, even the overhead smash. It is important to practice these shots until you have good placement and direction and the necessary power for each shot, which will give you overall proficiency and skill. After this has been accomplished, you can utilize these shots with certain variations and combinations by using sidewalls, front wall, and ceiling in order to gain the advantage over your opponent.

Kill Shot

This shot is probably the most effective one. It is utilized to terminate play, as the ball comes off the front wall so low and fast that it is impossible to return.

In order to execute a good kill shot, the ball should be hit from a low position off the floor. Any ball hit above the waist will be difficult to place in a kill position off the front wall. Also, it is important that you have enough time to get into the proper stroking position in order to put plenty of force into the shot. Many beginning players attempt to kill too many balls. Proper court position will be the determining factor in whether to use a kill shot.

Front Wall Kill (Fig. 3.1)

This shot is hit directly to the front wall in a straight line and rebounds in a straight line. This is the most-used kill shot, as it can be hit along either sidewall.

Pinch Shot Kill (Fig. 3.2)

This shot strikes the sidewall and then the front wall so that the rebound of the ball is away from the opponent. The amount of angle on the shot is determined by where the ball is hit on the sidewall. As in all kill shots, you should hit the ball hard and low.

Front Wall-Sidewall Kill (Fig. 3.3)

This is not as effective as the other kill shots because the ball has a higher bounce from hitting the sidewall. Also, the rebound will be toward your opponent, so the ball must be hit extremely low.

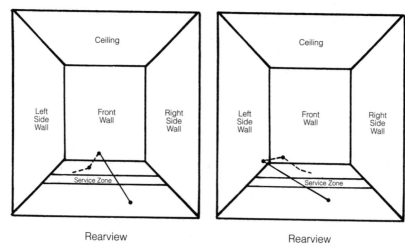

Rearview   Rearview

Figure 3.1
Front wall kill

Figure 3.2
Pinch shot kill

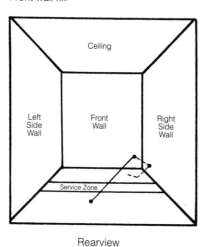

Rearview

Figure 3.3
Front wall-sidewall kill

Passing Shots (Fig. 3.4)

This is the most frequently used shot in racquetball. It can be hit when you are forced to swing faster than usual at the ball and when it is not possible to get into a set position. The basic principle behind this shot is to have the ball rebound from the front wall at such an angle that it will pass your opponent (fig. 3.4). The ball should be hit low enough so that it will not reach the back wall and preferably it should be struck at such an angle off the front wall that the ball will not hit either sidewall.

The passing shot should be used whenever your opponent is out of position. It is especially effective when an opponent is in the frontcourt or near the front wall.

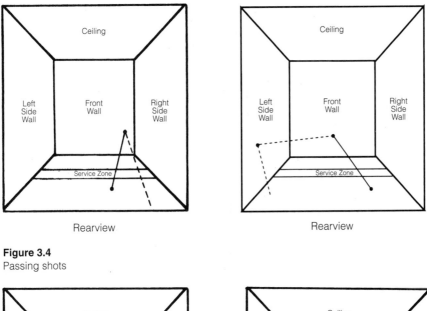

Figure 3.4
Passing shots

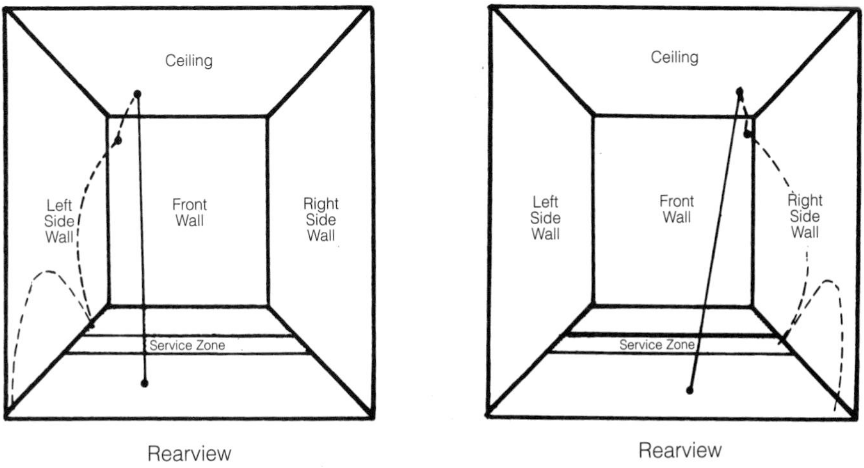

Figure 3.5
Ceiling shots

It is possible to use a wide-angle passing shot that is hit crosscourt and then strikes the sidewall at a point even with or slightly deeper than your opponent. If it contacts the sidewall farther up than this, the shot loses power and gives the opponent time to recover and return the ball. This type of passing shot requires accuracy and practice.

Ceiling Shot (Fig. 3.5)

The ceiling shot is most effective whenever you find your opponent in the front-court position and want to force your opponent to move into the backcourt. If hit properly with the right amount of speed and direction, it should force an opponent to retreat to the backcourt and to the back corner where the player will have difficulty making a strong return. The shot can be made from anywhere on the court, but it ideally is used from the center and backcourt areas.

The ball should be hit upward to contact the ceiling approximately three to six feet away from the front wall at such an angle that after hitting the ceiling, it will rebound sharply to the front wall and then rebound very high off the floor. With the proper rebound, the ball should come toward the back wall with a high arch, angling close to the sidewall and into the corner. The main objective is to get the ball to rebound with a high loft and a sharp drop to the corner or back wall.

The ceiling shot may be hit in more of a stand-up position, waist high or higher, and still be effective.

Lob Shot

The lob shot is similar to the ceiling shot except that the front wall is hit first. The ball is placed high on the front wall so that the rebound will come off close to the ceiling. Upon hitting the floor, the ball will rebound with a high arch and land close to the rear corner and back wall. It is important for you to remember on this shot to keep the ball as close to the sidewall as possible. This will make a return difficult for your opponent.

The purpose of the shot, as in the ceiling shot, is to move the opponent into the backcourt and thereby gain position and advantage.

Dropshot

The dropshot can be used most effectively when an opponent is caught close to the back wall and deep in backcourt position. It should be directed to the front corners in such a way that it will drop sharply into the corners with very little rebound.

What is the most frequently used shot in racquetball and when should it be tried? Where should your opponent be when you try the following shots: ceiling shot, lob shot, drop shot?

The objective is to make an opponent run the full distance of the court in order to return a ball that has little rebound. It should be remembered that the shot must be hit firmly by the racquet, but that the swing is checked immediately after the impact; there is very little follow-through. The shot can also be accomplished by using the overhead smash, but once again, the placement must be close or low to the front wall and into the corners.

Back Wall Play

This shot is probably harder to master than the normal forehand and backhand strokes, as it does require a turn to the back wall, pivoting to be in a position to hit the ball coming off the back wall. It requires great concentration in order to successfully stroke the ball. This shot is unusual in that you will hit the ball with the flow that, if executed properly, can result in great power and low placement.

The important thing to remember in making the back wall play is to position yourself properly for the shot so that you don't have to reach or run after the ball. It is imperative that you watch the ball closely during its flight to the back wall and as you make your turn toward the back wall in preparing for the shot. As you make the turn in the same direction that the ball is traveling, you must be prepared to immediately reverse your turn again and to pivot to the proper position facing the sidewall in order to make the forehand or backhand stroke. As you turn and pivot with the ball as it comes off the back wall, you will get the necessary speed and power required to return the ball to the front wall with good placement. It is important as the ball comes off the rear wall that you position yourself far enough away from the wall and the ball to get a good swing at it and to allow the ball to drop to the desired knee-high position. As in your normal forehand or backhand stroke, you start your backswing as soon as you start your pivot in relation to the ball and as the ball approaches you. You will step forward to the front wall with your lead foot and execute your forward swing, following through in the same manner as you would in hitting the normal shot. The important thing in this shot is to hit from a low position in order to make a solid and powerful ground stroke. As you follow through with the completion of the stroke, your body will now be pulled around so that you are facing the front wall and moving your feet to get into the "ready" position.

A shot off the back wall can be very powerful. Why is this, and what are the key points to remember in executing the shot?

More Difficult Shots and Serves

After you have mastered the basic shots you can now combine them into many combinations and variations. These possible modifications arise in a game due to the different court positions of an opponent.

Soft Corner Dropshot (Fig. 3.6)

This shot can be directed to either the front wall or the sidewall with the idea of hitting the ball close to the corner. The shot can be used with both the forehand and backhand strokes. It is also quite effective with the overhead smash. In using the soft corner dropshot, one must have good control of the ball and should not use a complete follow-through of the stroke. The ball is hit firmly but much softer than a regular shot. This creates a short rebound or short drop on the front or sidewall toward the corner.

Reverse Pinch Shot (Fig. 3.7)

This shot is most effective when the opponent is behind and to one side of you. Until you have completed a full swing on the ball, the opponent must usually wait before moving into recovery position. A greater angle off the sidewall will be used than in the corner dropshot.

This shot should be hit with good power and low enough on the sidewall so that it will rebound from the sidewall to the front wall in a low flight and then come off the front wall with a low bounce. If this shot is to be effective, the ball should never hit the sidewall above three feet; otherwise its rebound will angle off the front wall and will be high enough that the opponent will be able to reach it without any difficulty.

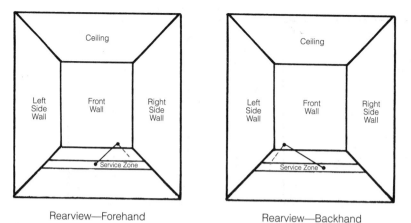

Rearview—Forehand   Rearview—Backhand

Figure 3.6
Soft corner dropshot

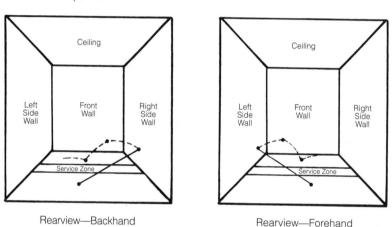

Rearview—Backhand   Rearview—Forehand

Figure 3.7
Reverse pinch shot

Crack Serve (Fig. 3.8)

In executing the crack serve, the ball is directed to the front wall about two to three feet to the side of center. The flight of the ball should come back over the front line and hit the junction of the sidewall and the floor at the same time. This must be a hard and fast shot. A good crack serve will not rebound high enough to allow a good return.

Diagonal Serve (Fig. 3.9)

At times you may find the opponent playing toward the corner of the backcourt in order to be in position to play an expected drive or lob serve. In order to keep the opponent honest, it is a good idea to change serves when this occurs. A serve that is effective against this strategy is the diagonal serve.

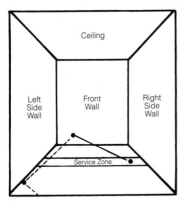

Figure 3.8
Crack serve

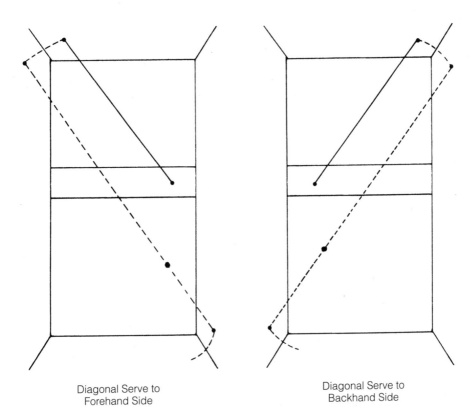

Diagonal Serve to
Forehand Side

Diagonal Serve to
Backhand Side

Figure 3.9
Diagonal serve

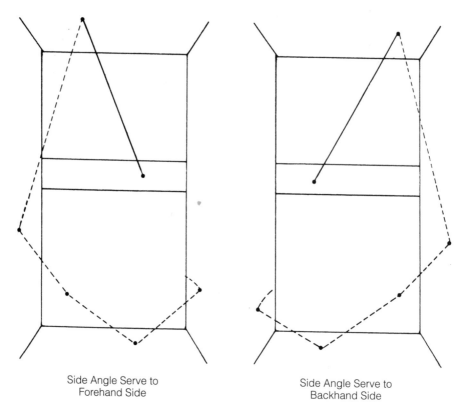

Side Angle Serve to
Forehand Side

Side Angle Serve to
Backhand Side

Figure 3.10
Side angle serve

In executing this serve, the ball should be hit to the front wall approximately three feet from the sidewall. The ball will then rebound from the front wall with good speed to the sidewall and will bounce into the backcourt and then rebound into the back corner.

This serve can be used in two different ways. The first method is to hit the ball hard, fast, and low off the front wall, which causes it to come out of the back corner extremely fast. This makes it difficult for an opponent to return the serve. In the second method, the ball can be hit much higher and slower off the front wall. This will cause the ball to have a more immediate and sharper drop into the back corner.

In either case, once the ball gets close to the back corner it will be extremely difficult for an opponent to make an effective return.

Side Angle Serve (Fig. 3.10)

This serve is hit relatively low and quite hard. The ball should be sent to the front wall close to the center and approximately three to four feet from the floor; it will then rebound to the sidewall about three to four feet back of the short line. The ball

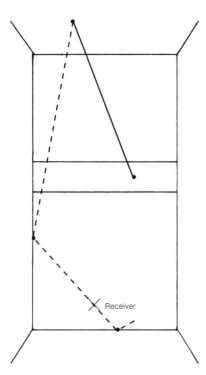

Figure 3.11
Jam serve

will then come out from the sidewall very quickly and continue on back to the back wall diagonally toward the opposite corner where the ball will now bounce to the opposite sidewall. On the final rebound, the ball will come off very close to this opposite sidewall and will drop to the floor close enough to the wall so that a return becomes quite difficult.

As you become proficient in racquetball, you will learn which shots to use in various situations. Once the various strokes have been mastered so accuracy of placement can be depended upon, you are ready to play top-level racquetball.

Jam Serve (Fig. 3.11)

Another variation of the side angle serve is called the "jam" serve. In this serve the ball comes off the sidewall fast and directly into the receiver in order to force a weak return of the serve.

Select from this chapter one of the types of serves described. Can you successfully execute this serve to the forehand and to the backhand side 3 times out of 10? 5 out of 10? 7 out of 10? Check your performance on other types of serves by the same standards.

Progress Can Be Speeded Up

4

In order to speed up progress in racquetball, you can engage in individual practice and general body conditioning. You may have excellent shots, but if you don't have the strength and endurance to execute them over a period of time during a match, then your chances of winning will decrease. Not only will a player's ability as a racquetball player be improved by practice but also the general strength and cardiorespiratory endurance will be beneficially affected.

Conditioning

Racquetball requires a great deal of strength and endurance, especially in the legs. It is estimated that a player travels about 1.5 miles in an average racquetball game. Following are some recommended exercises for racquetball.

1. *Rope Jumping.* This develops leg strength and endurance and also increases your agility.
2. *Running.* A good combination to use is jogging and wind sprints. You should attempt to reach the point where you can jog for a mile, do wind sprints (run fifty yards, jog fifty yards) for a half-mile, and then jog a half-mile.
3. *Shuffle Exercise.* In this exercise, assume a position as shown in figure 2.2 (see page 16). The knees are flexed and you shuffle in various directions as if playing in a racquetball game. Work to reach the point where this drill can be done for over ten minutes without stopping.
4. *Finger Push-Ups.* This exercise strengthens the muscles used in the various strokes.
5. *Finger Flip.* Stand upright with your arms extended outward from the sides. Flip your fingers as fast and hard as you can fifty times. Then extend your arms over your head and repeat the exercise fifty times. This is followed with the arms stretched in front of the chest; repeat again, fifty times. This strengthens the muscles used in the majority of racquetball strokes, especially those muscles of the forearm.
6. *Sit-Ups.* This exercise is done in a supine position with the hands behind the neck and the knees in a flexed position. The feet are in contact with the floor, but not stabilized by hooking them under a weighted object. Flexing the trunk, the player then attempts to touch the chest to thighs. If the resistance is too great, it can be reduced by placing the arms alongside the body while doing sit-ups. This is an excellent exercise to develop the abdominal muscles.

7. *Body Control.* In order to become a good racquetball player, you must have control of your body. The foundation for successful racquetball is the ability to quickly start, stop, change direction, change speed, and maneuver.

Prepare a Shuffle Exercise score card on which you can record your endurance time for each practice session on this exercise. What is your time for your first practice, for your second, etc., until you reach 10 seconds?

The ability to control the center of gravity is a key factor in body control. A normal stance used in racquetball is one with the knees flexed and the feet comfortably spread.

A good drill to develop body control is to line up chairs in rows about six feet apart. Run through these obstacles, varying your speed and direction. A variation using this same drill is to run toward a chair, fake to the left, and then run to the right.

There are many other exercises that you can engage in to develop strength and endurance. If more information is desired it is recommended that you obtain a book on conditioning or contact a reliable physical educator.

Individual Practice

It is important to remember that a person can learn bad habits as well as good habits. Too often the bad habits that one learns during practice come back to destroy the chance of winning during a match or tournament.

The objective that a person is trying to obtain through practice is to be able to make the shots without a lot of conscious effort. In order to develop the nervous system pathways necessary for racquetball skills, the body must experience the basic movements properly many times. The basic fundamentals are the keys to becoming an outstanding player. Whenever you go into the practice court you should have planned ahead what your practice is going to consist of. Just hitting shots at random, without a plan of attack, will not bring about the improvement that you desire.

In all individual practice sessions one should attempt to make the situation as similar to a game as possible. Many times players practice at half-speed and then find that all of this time was wasted when they try to adjust to an actual match situation.

Following are some individual drills that will be helpful in developing the basic skills necessary for racquetball.

The authors wish to express appreciation to Margaret Varner Bloss and Norman Bramall, authors of *Badminton and Squash Racquets* in the Brown & Benchmark Sports and Fitness series, for the basic ideas utilized in these drills.

Individual Drills

Racquetball is a game in which you can practice many of the shots individually, that is without the help of a partner. The broken line (__ __) on each drill indicates a setup. A setup places the ball in the correct location so that a specific shot can be

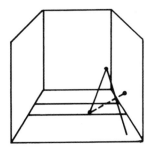

Figure 4.1
Wall shot drill

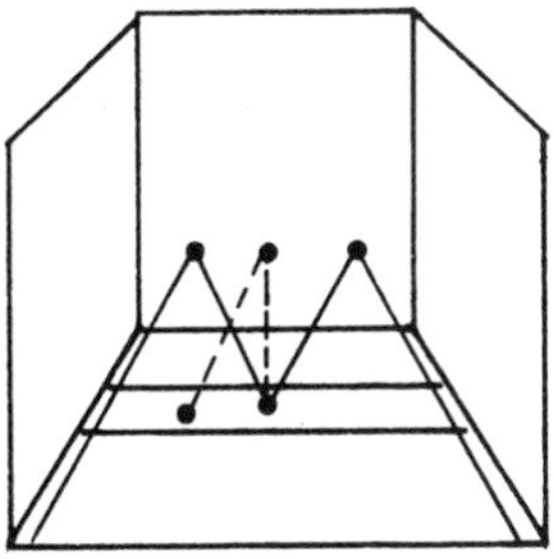

Figure 4.2
Forecourt wall shot and crosscourt shot drill

practiced. The dot represents the contact point of the ball and racquet. The continuous line (_____) is the desired direction and angle of the shot being practiced.

Wall Shot Drill (Fig. 4.1)

Setup Toss the ball about head height onto the sidewall near the front wall and let it bounce to the floor.
Object To stroke a forehand or backhand drive parallel to the sidewall with control.
Hints Note closely the angle the ball takes to and from the front wall. Begin with a short swing and gradually move back in the court as proficiency increases. Use both sides of the court.

Forecourt Wall Shot and Crosscourt Shot Drill (Fig. 4.2)

Setup Hit the ball any place on the front wall.
Object To play a wall shot or crosscourt shot from the area in the front court.
Hints Note the height of the drive on the front wall, which is necessary in order to get correct length. Use both backhand and forehand strokes. Gradually move back as accuracy increases.

Ceiling Shot Drill

Setup Hit the ball on the front wall so that it rebounds into the backcourt.
Object To hit a ceiling shot from a defensive position in the playing court.
Hints Hit the ceiling shot so that it is close to the sidewall and deep in the court without rebounding off the back wall or make sure it rebounds no higher than two feet. Emphasize control without swinging the racquet too hard. As you improve, attempt to hit the ceiling shots in a continuous drill.

Backcourt Wall Shot and Crosscourt Shot Drill (Fig. 4.3)

Setup Serve the ball so it rebounds off the back wall.
Object To play a wall shot or crosscourt drive from a defensive position in deep court.

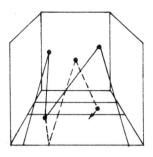

Figure 4.3
Backcourt wall shot and crosscourt shot drill

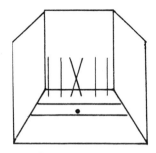

Figure 4.4
Volley drill

Hints To get depth, move towards the back wall and follow the ball as it goes to and from the back wall. Use both backhand and forehand strokes. Vary the drive with a lob.

Volley Drill (Fig. 4.4)

Setup Toss the ball to yourself and forehand volley it to the front wall and then volley continuously.

Object To increase reflex action. Begin by starting away from the front wall and gradually move closer to increase the tempo.

Hints Volley with a straight forehand first, then a backhand. As skill increases, crosscourt the volleys. Vary positions toward the sidewalls to make the drill more gamelike.

Back Wall Drill

Setup Serve the ball to the back wall. It may or may not hit the sidewall before the back wall.

Object To learn the action of a ball rebounding off the back wall. As proficiency develops, vary the speed and direction of the setup.

Hints Practice all of the shots on this type of setup.

Kill Shot (Fig. 4.5)

Setup Hit the ball any place on the front wall.

Object To play a kill shot from various areas of the playing court. Use both the forehand and backhand.

Hints Allow the ball to return so that it is only about 12 inches from the floor. Hit the ball low on the front wall so that it returns close to the floor.

Overhead Kill Shot (Fig. 4.6)

Setup Stand in the backcourt and hit a ceiling shot that bounces high into the backcourt.

Object To hit an overhead kill shot to the front wall.

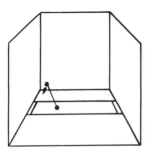

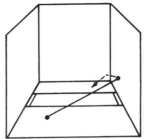

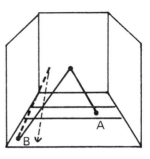

Figure 4.5
Kill shot

Figure 4.6
Overhead kill shot

Figure 4.7
Serve and return of serve drill

Hints Hit the ball down toward either of the front corners. You want to stroke the ball so that it hits either the front or sidewall close to the corner, thereby causing the ball to die so your opponent cannot return it. Aim for the crack of the front and sidewall, close to the floor.

Partner Drills

A great deal of improvement can be rapidly gained by working with another player. Repetition in hitting many specific types of shots will have a good carry-over to a game situation.

Serve and Return of Serve Drill (Fig. 4.7)

Description Serve and repeat a particular serve until it is effective. A particular type of return should also be practiced. Notice that some serves force the receiver to make a certain type of return.

The two shots utilized most often in racquetball are the serve and the return of serve. They should be practiced until good skill is acquired.

As you practice, can you and your partner stroke the ball crosscourt 10 times without missing? 15 times? 25 times? Can you do the same when you and your partner have changed sides of the court?

Crosscourt Shot Drill (Fig. 4.8)

Description A and B are in position to warm up. These positions can be moved forward and back in order to crosscourt the ball repeatedly and to hit the opposite sidewall anywhere behind the service area. A partner should return the ball with a drive or volley before it hits the sidewall. Change positions with a partner in order to practice both the forehand and backhand.
Hints Learn to play the ball at various heights on the front wall with varying amounts of speed.

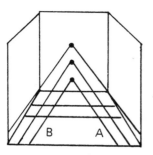

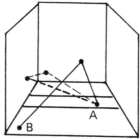

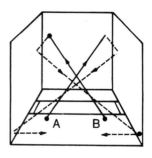

Figure 4.8
Crosscourt shot drill

Figure 4.9
Crosscourt drive and reverse
pinch drill

Figure 4.10
Repetitive Z-shot drill

Crosscourt Drive and Reverse Pinch Drill (Fig. 4.9)

Description A and B agree that one will crosscourt and the other will crosscorner.
After a few minutes change shots and also change sides to practice the
forehand and backhand of both shots.

Hints Elevate the crosscourt drive. The other player can then volley the ball down
the wall or crosscorner.

Repetitive Z-Shot Drill (Fig. 4.10)

Description Stand at mid-court with A and B on opposite sides. A player starts the
drill by dropping the ball and hitting a forehand Z-shot. The other player returns
the shot by using a backhand Z-shot. A and B can change sides after a given
number of shots in order to practice both the backhand and forehand Z-shots.

Hints The usual tendency in hitting a Z-shot is to contact it too low or too wide.
This type of shot will rebound into the center court and set up your opponent
for an easy shot. The ball should be hit in the front corner and high on the front
wall. A perfect Z-shot returns to the sidewall deep enough to have a bounce
that is parallel and close to the back wall.

Four-Stroke Drill

Description This drill makes the practice gamelike. The effectiveness of the first
three or four shots involved in a point should be analyzed.

Hints The quality of the serve and the return of the serve set the pattern the play
will take. Shots breaking off the sidewall and into the center of the court allow
an opponent to maintain the center position.

Summary

Although drills are helpful in speeding up progress, the best way to become an excellent racquetball player is to play as often as possible. After each game, attempt to analyze the quality of shots and the effectiveness of the strategy. Much energy can be saved by combining physical effort with thinking.

Repeating a stroke correctly over and over will eventually allow you to feel comfortable with a specific racquetball shot, but it is far different to practice shots than it is to hit the same shot under the stress, fatigue, and quick movements that are found in actual match situations.

As you rally prior to a game, what information should you try to obtain about your opponent's play, and how can you get it? Can you make use of this information during the game?

Patterns of Play

5

It is now time to bring together all the information about the racquetball strokes and use it as a basis to play a match.

Many beginning racquetball players have the false assumption that the best way to beat their opponent is to hit the ball as hard as possible. In order to become a proficient player you must know court position and specific patterns of play. This chapter will cover singles, doubles, and cutthroat games.

Court Position

It may be that the single most important factor in being a good racquetball player is court positioning. By being in the proper court position, you will be able to carry out your game plan, be ready to kill or return your opponent's shots, eliminate unnecessary steps and thus reduce the chance of early fatigue in the match, and be in an offensive position that will allow you to control the game and thus hit a higher percentage of winning shots.

The proper court position depends on the situation, but in most cases you should attempt to maintain a position on the playing court referred to as the center court area. This area extends from just behind the back service line to about 9 feet from the back wall and to within 2 to 3 feet of both sidewalls. Figure 5.1 contains a presentation of the center court area.

One of the chief reasons for controlling this center court area is that any ball hit with a sufficient amount of velocity to strike a sidewall, either on the way to or returning from the front wall, will angle toward the middle of the court. If you are not in the center court area, you will need a perfect kill shot or an unreachable pass shot to make contact with most of your opponent's return shots.

By learning to play in this court area, you will always be only one or two steps away from the majority of balls that your opponent can hit. The biggest mistake most beginners make is to play too close to the front wall, and thus find themselves in a poor court position.

You will want to start to think of the center court area as your home base. After nearly every shot, force yourself to return to this area. A good method to practice this style of play is to find a friend who will play a match with you. Then tape an X directly in the middle of the center court area. This will give you a visual reference point to check as you play the game.

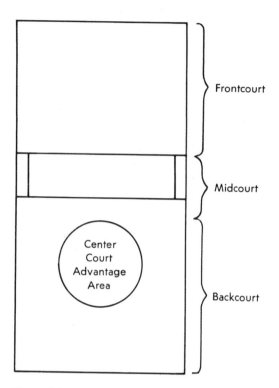

Figure 5.1
Center court advantage area

It should be pointed out that control of center court is being sought by both you and your opponent. Both players are usually in that area, jockeying for court position with the shots they hit. Therefore, your ability to hit the fundamental shots will also determine your ability to control the center court area.

You want to keep yourself in center court position, but you also want to keep the shots that you hit to your opponent out of center court.

Singles Strategy

Server (Fig. 5.2)

When serving in singles, the rule states that the server must be within the confines of the service zone. (For complete information on serving, refer to the serve rules beginning on page 27.) In most cases, it is recommended that the server stand at the center of the service zone. This allows the best angles to both back corners and provides you with the most options of the places you might wish to serve the ball.

After completing the serve and after most shots, you should move immediately to the center court area. Have you made this return to home base an automatic action? Try keeping a mental record for each 10 strokes of the number of times you succeed in reaching home base.

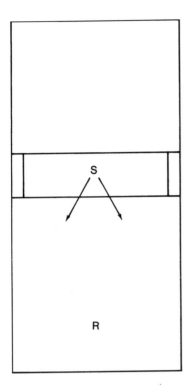

Figure 5.2
Single serving and receiving positions

After serving, take a couple of steps behind the short line. By doing this, you will be moving into a position that will enable you to control the center court area.

If you've served to the left, step behind the short line and approximately one step toward the left wall. If the serve is to the right, then move behind the short line and one step toward the right wall. See figure 5.2 for an example of these positions.

As you move to these positions, angle your body so that you can watch your opponent. For example, if you have served into the left back corner, your feet will be pointing toward the left front corner. A slight turn of the head will now allow you to observe your opponent set up and begin to swing for the return shot. This will allow you to anticipate and react rapidly for your return shot. A player who faces straight toward the front wall will usually be caught flat-footed and in poor position for the return.

In serving, there are two body levels to serve from. These are known as the low zone and the high zone. The low zone is where the server contacts the ball from a height approximately between the mid-calf and the knee. This level includes the drive serves and the low Z-serves. The attempt is to use a serve that will elicit a weak service return that can be put away by the server. If there is a problem serving from this zone, it is the difficulty of accuracy; an inaccurate serve may rebound off the back wall for an easy return.

The high zone is the body area that is mid-thigh to chest high. The type of serves used in this zone are the lob serve and the high Z-serves. The attempt of serves in this zone is to put the ball into play without making an error on the serve. Serves from this zone usually do not elicit a weak return, so there is a longer rally before a point is won.

You should be aware of your opponent's weakness in regard to the serve and use the shots that are most strategically sound. Changing the type of serve during the course of play can lead to confusion within the mind of the receiver, and thus keep the receiver in a defensive court position.

Most racquetball players are most successful when they put the ball in play by serving to their opponent's backhand.

As stated previously, the drive serve is the most effective serve. The ball should come off the left center side of the front wall so that the rebound will come back fast and low, clearing the short line while in flight and coming as close as possible and parallel to the left sideline, so that the opponent does not have an opportunity to get an open shot at the serve.

After the server has completed the serve, remember that it is important not to just stand still. The rule states that the server must stay within the service zone until the served ball has passed over the short line. Immediately after this, the server should be stepping back of the short line to establish a playing position that will enable the server to have control of center court.

Receiver (Fig. 5.2)

As with the serve, the important factor concerning the service return is center court positioning. The receiver's position in singles should be one that is in the center of the rear court and about 3 to 5 feet in front of the back wall. From this position, the receiver can cover either side of the court and thus cut down the chance of being aced on the serve.

A player should at all times assume the ready position. The player's feet should be spread approximately shoulder width, parallel with each other. The knees should be slightly bent so that the weight is shifted toward the balls of the feet. The body should be straight and the head up, watching the front court in order to see the flight of the ball as it comes off the front wall.

The goal of the receiver is to achieve the center court position controlled by the server. Since the receiver is located in the backcourt, the logical means of forcing the server to exchange court positions is by means of a defensive shot. To do this, the receiver might use a ceiling shot or pass shot to force the server to move out of the center court area. Then the receiver moves in and by switching positions, the receiver has gained the advantage. Figure 3.5 (see pg. 43) contains an explanation of how a ceiling shot along the left wall might be used against a drive serve to the left.

Also, the receiver can anticipate the type of serve that might be expected by observing the body zone the server uses to make contact with the ball. If the ball is hit in the low zone, then anticipate and prepare for a low drive serve or a low Z-serve.

If the ball is hit in the high zone, then the receiver can move up and take the ball on the fly before it hits the floor, providing the receiver does not violate the safety

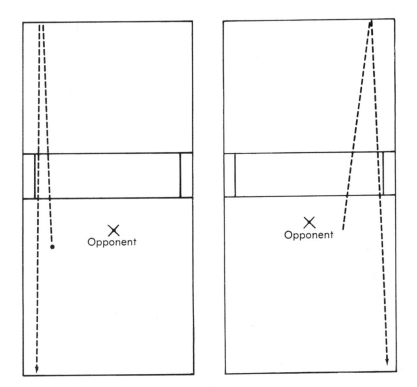

Figure 5.3
Backhand down the line pass and forehand down the line pass

zone regulations. Anytime you can hit the ball on the fly, you won't always have to hit a perfect passing shot or kill shot, as the server will still be standing in the service zone and in many cases the ball will be past the server before he can react.

It is important to remember to hit the ball away from your opponent and make your opponent move wherever possible. It is much more difficult to hit a ball when in motion.

Rallying

As has been emphasized before, you will want to keep yourself in center court position and you will want to keep your shots out of your opponent's center court. A shot that passes through the center court area gives your opponent the best opportunity to hit the ball without having to run for the ball in order to make contact and also forces you to leave center court to give room for your opponent.

A key point is to hit the ball away from your opponent. As your ability to hit the ball with control increases, make yourself aware of where your opponent is during the rally and force your opponent to run the farthest possible distance to retrieve your shot. A common error made by many beginners in racquetball is to try to hit the ball too hard and thus hit the ball through their opponent. The key is to hit the ball around the opponent. Figure 5.3 contains an example of this type of strategy.

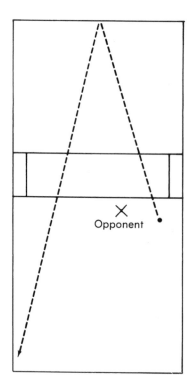
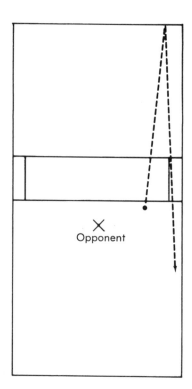

Figure 5.4
Crosscourt shot away from the opponent

Figure 5.5
Kill shot down the wall

One helpful hint is to hit the ball crosscourt while rallying with an opponent. This type of shot will prevent the ball from going straight to the back wall and then rebounding into the center court area, allowing your opponent to make an easy return on your shot. By hitting the ball crosscourt, you can force your opponent out of the center court area and thus you can gain control of this area. Figure 5.4 explains how to utilize this tactic in playing racquetball.

On rallies where your opponent is behind you, one of the best shots to use is a kill shot down the wall. It is very difficult to cover the area of the wall, and the ball will carry to the back corner and thus force your opponent out of center court. In order to hit this shot, when you are in center court, you should aim for a spot on the front wall that is about 5 feet from the sidewall. Even though you may hit some balls that still go through center court, you will still win many points because the added speed of the kill shot will make it more difficult to hit. Figure 5.5 contains a description of this type of playing strategy.

As the receiver, what is the advantage you gain by hitting the ball on the fly when possible?

When you find yourself forced out of the center court area and in the back-court, the two best shots to use are a passing shot or a ceiling shot. It is difficult to hit a kill shot from the backcourt unless you have spent considerable time practic-ing this shot. The passing shot is usually hit to the backhand, as this will probably be the weakest stroke of your opponent. The ceiling shot should be hit in such a manner as to force your opponent to run to hit the ball in the back court. In executing the shots, it is important to try to hit a shot that does not strike the sidewall. After you have made your shot, you should always attempt to move to center court.

By combining the strategy of maintaining center court position and good shot selection, you should now be able to force your opponent to hit shots that you can take at the front and mid-court areas. This will allow you to be in control of the game and thus develop a winning racquetball style.

Doubles Strategy

There are many excellent features to the game of doubles in racquetball. It provides a good change of pace from the singles game; it allows you to combine a team aspect to racquetball; it is a means of having a coeducational type of game by playing mixed doubles; and it is less strenuous than singles, but still a very enjoyable experience.

Playing together as a unit is not too difficult if the two partners decide in advance what type of basic court position and strategy they will follow. A communication system should be used, so that one partner will call the shots during the rally so there are no questions as to which partner will return a given shot. An effective method to provide this information, concerning who is responsible for a shot return, is to use a simple "yours" or "mine." To reduce conflict and error during the course of play, it is best to designate one partner who will be responsible to call each ball throughout the match.

Can you recall several tips for effective placement of your shots?

Side-by-Side Formation (Fig. 5.6)

This is the most logical and efficient formation to use in playing doubles. In this formation, each player has the responsibility for one half of the court. If it is ever necessary for one player to get out of position, then the teammate shifts into the vacant area to cover the shot.

If a team is composed of one player who is right-handed and another player who is left-handed, then this allows the team to cover the passing lanes and serving areas with forehand shots. The possible weak area would be to decide who will cover shots down the middle. If possible, the player with the strongest backhand should take these shots.

Modified Side-by-Side Formation (Fig. 5.7)

Since most teams will be composed of two right-handed players, the modified side-by-side formation is a good style of play to use. The player with the best backhand will play the left side of the court and the right-side player has a major responsibility in covering the right front corner, as this is a potential area for scoring points.

What are your specific responsibilities as a right court doubles player using the modified side-by-side system of court coverage? As the left court player?

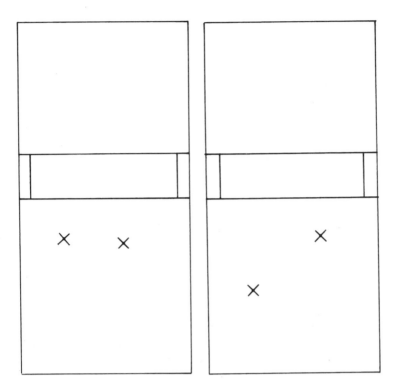

Figure 5.6
Side-by-side formation

Figure 5.7
Modified side-by-side formation

The left-side player generally plays a little deeper to protect the backhand, and this sets up a diagonal formation for court coverage. By doing this, you are now utilizing the strengths of both partners.

I-Formation or Front/Back Formation (Fig. 5.8)

The basic idea behind this formation is to have one player up and the other player back. This formation requires players with some special and unique playing skills. The front player has to be especially quick, very aggressive in covering the court, and have good skill in retrieving the ball. He or she also has to have the ability to hit good kill shots. The back player has to be skilled in hitting the ball from the deep court and has to be especially able to hit the ceiling shot with good control. Also the back player must have good ability to play the ball off the back wall.

What advantage is gained when one doubles partner is right-handed and the other is left-handed? What is the disadvantage and how can it be overcome?

Center Court Strategy

As in singles, control of the center court area is required in order to produce a winning game of doubles. By controlling the center court, your team is in the best position to return the majority of the opposing team's shots. Your team will be hitting

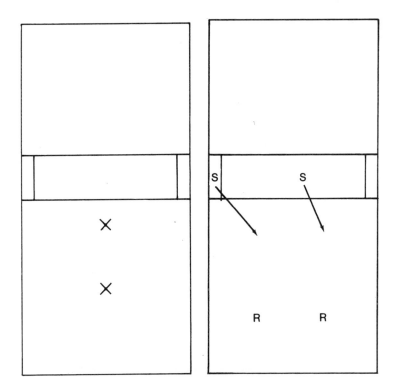

Figure 5.8
I-Formation—front/back formation

Figure 5.9
Doubles serving and receiving positions

shots that are closer to the front wall, and thus you will increase the chance of hitting a more accurate shot. It is also much easier to see the ball when your opponents are behind you and not partially blocking your view of the shot. And finally, since you usually don't have to hit a shot around another player, you have the opportunity to hit a wider variety of kill shots without the problem of hitting your opponent with the ball.

The serving team should use serves that will allow them to maintain a center court position, and the receiving team should always try to return the serve in such a way that the opposition will be forced away from the center court area.

Servers (Fig. 5.9)

In doubles, the partner of the server must be within the confines of the server's box. The server is in the same basic position in the service zone as in singles. The server's partner must stay within the service box until the ball has hit the front wall and has come back and crossed the short line. After this has happened, both the server and the partner should move to control the center court area.

Proper serving is an important part of the doubles game. You should aim for the back corners, the same as in singles. In doubles, though, accuracy is more important than power. A Z-serve to the weakest player is a good serve. A high lob serve that will cause a defensive return also works well in doubles. The thing to always keep in mind is to use a serve that will allow the serving team time to get into position to control the center court. In doubles, do not use a serve that will put your partner in a position that might cause an avoidable hinder. (See rules, chapter 6.)

Receivers (Fig. 5.9)

The receiving team should try to return the serve using a shot so that the opposing team is forced out of the center court area, and then they should move as quickly as possible to gain control of this area for themselves.

If the serve is hit poorly, make an aggressive return by attempting a kill shot or to drive the ball crosscourt. You may have to use a wider angle on the crosscourt shot so that you increase the chance of the ball going by your opponent. Attempt to have the ball hit the sidewall just behind the area of the court where your opponent is standing.

The volley shot, where you hit the serve before it bounces, can sometimes be used effectively against the lob serve. This will allow you to return the ball quicker and reduce the time that the serving team has to get to the center court area. The volley is not only a good shot against the serve, but it is also a good shot to use in doubles, as it decreases the time your opponents have to react to your shot.

When in doubt as to the stroke to use, either on the serve or during the course of play, go to the ceiling shot. This has excellent strategic value, as it may move your opponent out of center court position and give your team time to jockey for an offensive position. Patience is an important part of the doubles game. Many teams are not successful because they are not willing to wait until the proper time arrives to hit the correct shot. By using a defensive ceiling shot, your opponents may make an error or hit a low percentage shot, which will allow your team to put the ball away.

The key to successful doubles, of course, is to play the other team's weaknesses. Doubles can be a great game, and by playing doubles, you can develop a wide variety of playing skills. You can then plan a strategy of playing the game that employs the combined assets of the two partners to the best advantage.

Three Man or Cutthroat Strategy

In three man racquetball, the rules to follow in court position are simple. When serving, try to attain the position as explained for the singles game. When receiving, utilize the positions explained for the doubles game.

Why is a defensive ceiling shot a good choice when you are undecided as to which shot to use to make a return?

Language of Racquetball and the Rules of the Game

6

Common Racquetball Terms

Racquetball has developed in a short time into a game of national interest. Many of the terms and the language used in racquetball are similar to those used in handball, tennis, and squash. In order to understand and communicate with other racquetball players, the following list of terms is considered important.

Ace
A serve untouched by the receiver.

Advantage position—center court
The position on the court where a player can hit most shots and control the game. It is approximately five feet back of the short line in the middle of the court.

Avoidable hinder
Interference with an opponent during play, resulting in either a point or side out.

Backcourt
The area back of the short line.

Backhand
Hitting the ball from the nondominant side.

Backswing
Taking the racquet back in preparation for beginning the swing.

Blocking
Preventing the opponent from hitting the ball by moving some part of the body between the opponent and the ball.

Ceiling shot
A ball hit upward that contacts the ceiling approximately three to six feet away from the front wall at such an angle that after hitting the ceiling, it will rebound sharply to the front wall and then rebound very high off the floor toward the back wall.

Court
The playing area.

Court hinder
When play is hindered by a part of the playing court, such as the ball hitting a door handle or after striking a wet spot on the floor or wall, and in the referee's opinion the irregular bounce affects the rally.

Crotch ball
A ball hitting at the juncture of the service wall and the ceiling, floor, or sidewall or in the corners.

Cutthroat

A game involving three players with each player playing against the other two.

Dead ball

A ball that is no longer in play.

Defensive player

The receiver.

Doubles

Two players playing against two other players.

Drive

Hitting the ball hard to the front wall so that it rebounds on a relatively straight line.

Error

Failure to successfully return a ball during play.

Fault

An infraction of the service rule.

Follow-through

The continuation of the swing of the racquet after the ball has been hit.

Foot fault

Illegal position of the server's feet on the serve.

Forehand

Hitting the ball from the dominant side.

Frontcourt

The court area in front of the service line.

Game

The winning of fifteen points, constituting a game.

Half volley

Hitting the ball just after it bounces from the playing surface.

Handout

A loss of serve by the first server in doubles.

Hinder

Unintentional interference with an opponent during play, resulting in replay of point.

Illegal server

Failure to serve the ball in accordance with the playing rules.

Kill

A ball hit so low to the front wall that it is practically unplayable.

Lob

A ball hit high and gently to the front wall, which rebounds in a high arc to the back wall.

Match

The winning of two out of three games.

Offensive player

The server.

Out serve
A player losing the serve in accordance with the rules.

Pass
A ball hit to the side and out of the reach of an opponent.

Placement
A shot hit to the spot where it was intended.

Rally
The playing time between the serve and the end of the point.

Receiver
The receiver of the serve.

Rest period
Intervals during and between games in accordance with the rules.

Roll out
A ball that strikes the front wall so low that it simply "rolls out" on the floor.

Safety zone
Area of court between the short line and the receiving line and observed during the serve and return of serve.

Screen
Interference with opponent's vision in attempting to play the ball.

Screen ball
A ball that passes so close to a player that the receiver's view of the ball is obstructed; this ball should be replayed.

Screen serve
A served ball passing so close to the server's body on the rebound that the receiver is unable to pick up the flight of the ball. A screen serve results in a fault serve.

Server
The player hitting the ball to the front wall to begin the play of the point.

Service box
In doubles, the area in which the server's partner must remain until the serve has passed the short line.

Service line
In four-wall racquetball, a line parallel to and five feet in front of the short line. In one-wall racquetball, it is a line parallel to and nine feet back of the short line.

Service zone
The area between and including the service line and the short line.

Short
A serve failing to rebound past the short line.

Short line
In four-wall racquetball, a line midway between and parallel to the front and back walls. In one-wall racquetball, a line parallel to and sixteen feet from the front wall.

Sidelines
The lines marking left- and right-hand boundaries of the court in one-wall and three-wall racquetball.

Sideout
Loss of service by player in singles or both players in doubles.
Straddle ball
A ball going between the legs of a player.
Thong
A cord attached to the handle of a racquet to prevent the racquet from leaving a player's hand and causing injury.
Volley
Playing the ball in the air before it has bounced.

Can you explain what is meant by the following racquetball service terms: fault serves, out serves, dead-ball serves, drive service zones?

Rules of the Game

The rules governing racquetball are simple and easy to learn. The official rules are published by The American Amateur Racquetball Association, 1685 West Uintah, Colorado Springs, Colorado 80904–2921. The telephone number is (719) 635–5396.

1—The Game

1.1   Types of Games
1.2   Description
1.3   Objective
1.4   Points and Outs
1.5   Match, Game, Tiebreaker
1.6   Doubles Team
1.7   Consolation Matches

2—Courts and Equipment

2.1   Court Specifications
2.2   Ball Specifications
2.3   Ball Selection
2.4   Racquet Specifications
2.5   Apparel

3—Officiating

3.1   Tournament Management
3.2   Tournament Rules Committee
3.3   Referee Appointment and Removal
3.4   Rules Briefing
3.5   Referees

Rule Modifications

6.0   Eight and Under Multi-Bounce
7.0   One-Wall and Three-Wall Play
8.0   Wheelchair Racquetball
9.0   Visually Impaired Racquetball
10.0 Deaf Racquetball
11.0 Women's Pro Racquetball Association [WPRA]
12.0 International Racquetball Tour [Men's Pro]

1—The Game

Rule 1.1 Types of Games

Racquetball may be played by two or four players. When played by two it is called singles and when played by four, doubles. A non-tournament variation of the game that is played by three players is called cutthroat.

Rule 1.2 Description

Racquetball is a competitive game in which a strung racquet is used to serve and return the ball.

Rule 1.3 Objective

The objective is to win each rally by serving or returning the ball so the opponent is unable to keep the ball in play. A rally is over when a player (or team in doubles) is unable to hit the ball before it touches the floor twice, is unable to return the ball in such a manner that it touches the front wall before it touches the floor, or when a hinder is called.

Rule 1.4 Points and Outs

Points are scored only by the serving side when it serves an irretrievable serve (an ace) or wins a rally. Losing the serve is called a sideout in singles. In doubles, when the first server loses the serve it is called a handout; when the second server loses the serve it is a sideout.

Rule 1.5 Match, Game, Tiebreaker

A match is won by the first side winning two games. The first two games of a match are played to 15 points. If each side wins one game, a tiebreaker game is played to 11 points.

Rule 1.6 Doubles Team

(a)   A doubles team shall consist of two players who meet either the age requirements or player classification requirements to participate in a particular division of play. A team with different skill levels must play in the division of the player with the higher level of ability. When playing in an adult age division, the team must play in the division of the younger player. When playing in a junior age division, the team must play in the division of the older player.

(b) A change in playing partners may be made as long as the first match of the posted team has not begun. For this purpose only the match will be considered started once the teams have been called to the court. The team must notify the tournament director of the change prior to the beginning of the match.

Rule 1.7 Consolation Matches

(a) Each entrant shall be entitled to participate in a minimum of two matches. Therefore, losers of their first match shall have the opportunity to compete in a consolation bracket of their own division. In draws of less than seven players, a round robin may be offered. See Rule 5.5 about how to determine the winner of a round robin event.

(b) Consolation matches may be waived at the discretion of the tournament director, but this waiver must be in writing on the tournament application.

(c) Preliminary consolation matches will be two of three games to 11 points. Semifinal and final matches will follow the regular scoring format.

2—Courts and Equipment

Rule 2.1 Court Specifications (See figure 6.1.)

The specifications for the standard four-wall racquetball court are:

(a) Dimensions. The dimensions shall be 20 feet wide, 40 feet long and 20 feet high, with a back wall at least 12 feet high. All surfaces shall be in play, with the exception of any gallery opening or surfaces designated as court hinders.

(b) Markings. Racquetball courts shall be marked with lines 1½ inches wide as follows:

1. Short Line. The back edge of the short line is midway between, and is parallel with, the front and back walls.
2. Service Line. The front edge of the service line is parallel with, and five feet in front of, the back edge of the short line.
3. Service Zone. The service zone is the five-foot area between the outer edges of the short line and service line.
4. Service Boxes. The service boxes are located at each end of the service zone and are designated by lines parallel with the side walls. The edge of the line nearest to the center of the court shall be 18 inches from the nearest side wall.
5. Drive Serve Lines. The drive serve lines, which form the drive serve zone, are parallel with the side wall and are within the service zone. The edge of the line nearest to the center of the court shall be three feet from the nearest side wall.
6. Receiving Line. The receiving line is a broken line parallel to the short line. The back edge of the receiving line is five feet from the back edge of the short line. The receiving line begins with a line 21 inches long that extends from each side wall. These lines are connected by an alternate series of six-inch spaces and six-inch lines. This will result in a line composed of 17 six-inch spaces, 16 six-inch lines, and two 21-inch lines.

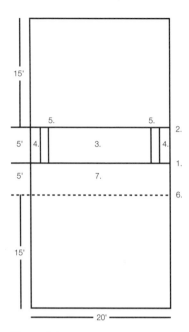

Figure 6.1
Court specifications

7. Safety Zone. The safety zone is the five-foot area bounded by the back edges of the short line and the receiving line. The zone is observed only during the serve. See Rules 4.11 (k) and 4.12.

Rule 2.2 Ball Specifications

(a) The standard racquetball shall be 2¼ inches in diameter; weigh approximately 1.4 ounces; have a hardness of 55–60 inches durometer; and bounce 68–72 inches from a 100-inch drop at a temperature of 70–74 degrees Fahrenheit.
(b) Only a ball having the endorsement or approval of the AARA may be used in an AARA sanctioned tournament.

Rule 2.3 Ball Selection

(a) A ball shall be selected by the referee for use in each match. During the match the referee may, at his discretion or at the request of a player or team, replace the ball. Balls that are not round or which bounce erratically shall not be used.
(b) If possible, the referee and players should agree to an alternate ball, so that in the event of breakage, the second ball can be put into play immediately.

Rule 2.4 Racquet Specifications

(a) The racquet, including bumper guard and all solid parts of the handle, may not exceed 21 inches in length.
(b) The racquet frame may be any material judged to be safe.

(c) The racquet frame must include a cord that must be securely attached to the player's wrist.
(d) The string of the racquet should be gut, monofilament, nylon, graphite, plastic, metal, or a combination thereof, providing the strings do not mark or deface the ball.
(e) Using an illegal racquet will result in forfeiture of the game in progress or, if discovered between games, forfeiture of the preceding game.

Rule 2.5 Apparel

(a) Effective September 1, 1995, lensed eyewear designed for racquetball, and which meets or exceeds ASTM F803 or Canadian (CSA) impact standards, is required apparel. This rule applies to all persons, including those who must wear corrective lenses. The eyewear must be worn as designed and at all times. A player who fails to wear proper eyewear will be assessed a technical foul and a timeout to obtain proper eyewear. A second infraction in the same match will result in immediate forfeiture of the match. (See Rule 4.18 (a)(9).) The current AARA Approved Eyewear List is available from the AARA's national office.
(b) Clothing and Shoes. The clothing may be of any color; however, a player may be required to change wet, extremely loose fitting, or otherwise distracting garments. Insignias and writing on the clothing must be considered to be in good taste by the tournament director. Shoes must have soles which do not mark or damage the floor.
(c) Equipment Requirements During Warm-up. Approved eyeguards must be worn and wrist cords must be used during any on-court warm-up period. The referee should give a technical warning to any person who fails to comply and assess a technical foul if that player continues to not comply after receiving such a warning.

3—Officiating

Rule 3.1 Tournament Management

All AARA sanctioned tournaments shall be managed by a tournament director, who shall designate the officials.

Rule 3.2 Tournament Rules Committee

The tournament director may appoint a tournament rules committee to resolve any disputes that the referee, tournament desk, or tournament director cannot resolve. The committee, composed of an odd number of persons, may include state or national officials, or other qualified individuals in attendance who are prepared to meet on short notice. The tournament director should not be a member of this committee.

Rule 3.3 Referee Appointment and Removal

The principal official for every match shall be the referee who has been designated by the tournament director, or his designated representative, and who has been agreed upon by all participants in the match. The referee's authority regarding a match begins once the players are called to the court. The referee may be removed from a match upon the agreement of all participants (teams in doubles) or at the discretion of the tournament director or his designated representative. In the event that a referee's removal is requested by one player or team and not agreed to by the other, the tournament director or his designated representative may accept or reject the request. It is suggested that the match be observed before determining what, if any, action is to be taken. In addition, two line judges and a scorekeeper may also be designated to assist the referee in officiating the match.

Rule 3.4 Rules Briefing

Before all tournaments, all officials and players shall be briefed on rules as well as local court hinders, regulations, and modifications the tournament director wishes to impose. The briefing should be reduced to writing. The current AARA rules will apply and be made available. Any modifications the tournament director wishes to impose must be stated on the entry form and be available to all players at registration.

Rule 3.5 Referees

(a) Pre-Match Duties. Before each match begins, it shall be the duty of the referee to:
1. Check on adequacy of preparation of court with respect to cleanliness, lighting and temperature.
2. Check on availability and suitability of materials to include balls, towels, scorecards, pencils and timepiece necessary for the match.
3. Check the readiness and qualifications of the line judges and scorekeeper. Review appeal procedures and instruct them of their duties, rules and local regulations.
4. Go onto the court to introduce himself and the players; brief the players on court hinders, local regulations, rule modifications for this tournament; explain misinterpreted rules.
5. Inspect players' equipment; identify the line judges; verify selection of a primary and alternate ball.
6. Toss coin and offer the winner the choice of serving or receiving.

(b) Decisions. During the match, the referee shall make all decisions with regard to the rules. Where line judges are used, the referee shall announce all final judgments. If both players in singles and three out of four in a doubles match disagree with a call made by the referee, the referee is overruled with the exception of technical fouls and forfeitures.

(c) Protests. Any decision not involving the judgment of the referee will, on protest, be accorded due process as set forth in the by-laws of the AARA. For the purposes of rendering a prompt decision regarding protests filed during the course of an ongoing tournament, the stages of due process will be first to the tournament director and second to the tournament rules committee. In those instances when time permits, the protest may be elevated to the state association and then to the National Board of Directors in the manner prescribed in the by-laws.

(d) Forfeitures. A match may be forfeited by the referee when:
1. Any player refuses to abide by the referee's decision or engages in unsportsmanlike conduct.
2. Any player or team who fails to report to play 10 minutes after the match has been scheduled to play. (The tournament director may permit a longer delay if circumstances warrant such a decision.)
(e) Defaults. A player or team may be forfeited by the tournament director or official for failure to comply with the tournament or host facility's rules while on the premises between matches, or for abuse of hospitality, locker room, or other rules and procedures.
(f) Spectators. The referee shall have jurisdiction over the spectators, as well as the players, while the match is in progress.
(g) Other Rulings. The referee may rule on all matters not covered in the AARA Official Rules. However, the referee's ruling is subject to protest as described in Rule 3.5 (c).

Rule 3.6 Line Judges

(a) When Utilized. Two line judges should be used for semifinal and final matches, when requested by a player or team, or when the referee or tournament director so desires. However, the use of line judges is subject to availability and the discretion of the tournament director.
(b) Replacing Line Judges. If any player objects to a person serving as a line judge before the match begins, all reasonable effort shall be made to find a replacement acceptable to the officials and players. If a player objects after the match begins, any replacement shall be at the discretion of the referee and/or tournament director.
(c) Position of Line Judges. The players and referee shall designate the court location of the line judges. Any dispute shall be settled by the tournament director.
(d) Duties and Responsibilities. Line judges are designated to help decide appealed calls. In the event of an appeal, and after a very brief explanation of the appeal by the referee, the line judges must indicate their opinion of the referee's call.
(e) Signals. Line judges should extend their arm and signal as follows: (i) thumb up to show agreement with the referee's call, (ii) thumb down to show disagreement, and (iii) hand open with palm facing down to indicate "no opinion" or that the play in question wasn't seen.
(f) Manner of Response. Line judges should be careful not to signal until the referee acknowledges the appeal and asks for a ruling. In responding to the referee's request, line judges should not look at each other, but indicate their opinions simultaneously in clear view of the players and referee. If at any time a line judge is unsure of which call is being appealed or what the referee's call was, the line judge should ask the referee to repeat the call and the appeal.
(g) Result of Response. If both line judges signal no opinion, the referee's call stands. If both line judges disagree with the referee, the referee must reverse the ruling. If one line judge agrees with the call and one disagrees, the referee's

call stands. If one line judge agrees with the call and one has no opinion, the call stands. If one line judge disagrees with the referee's call and the other signals no opinion, the rally is replayed. Any replays, with the exception of appeals on the second serve itself, will result in two serves.

Rule 3.7 Appeals

(a) Appealable Calls and Non-Calls. In any match using line judges, a player may appeal only the following calls or noncalls by the referee: skip ball; fault serve, except screen serves; out serve; double bounce pickup; receiving line violation; and court hinder. At no time may a player appeal a screen serve, a hinder call (except court hinders), a technical foul, or other discretionary call of the referee.

(b) How to Appeal. A verbal appeal by a player must be made directly to the referee immediately after the rally has ended. A player who believes there is an infraction to appeal, should bring it to the attention of the referee and line judges by raising his non-racquet hand at the time the perceived infraction occurs. The player is obligated to continue to play until the rally has ended or the referee stops play. The referee will recognize a player's appeal only if it is made before that player leaves the court for any reason including timeouts and game-ending rallies or, if that player doesn't leave the court, before the next serve begins.

(c) Loss of Appeal. A player or team forfeits its right of appeal for that rally if the appeal is made directly to the line judges or, if the appeal is made after an excessive demonstration or complaint.

(d) Limit on Appeals. A player or team may make three appeals per game. However, if either line judge disagrees (thumb down) with the referee's call, that appeal will not count against the three-appeal limit. In addition, the game-ending rally may be appealed even if the three-appeal limit has been reached.

Rule 3.8 Outcome of Appeals

(a) Skip Ball. If the referee makes a call of "skip ball," the call may be appealed. If the call is reversed, the referee then must decide if the shot in question could have been returned had play continued. If in the opinion of the referee, the shot could have been returned, the rally shall be replayed. However, if the shot was not retrievable, the side which hit the shot in question is declared the winner of the rally. If the referee makes no call on a shot (thereby indicating that the shot did not skip), an appeal may be made that the shot skipped. If the no call is reversed, the side which hit the shot in question loses the rally.

(b) Fault Serve. If the referee makes a call of fault serve, the call may be appealed. If the call is reversed, the serve is replayed, unless if the referee considered the serve to be not retrievable, in which case a point is awarded to the server. An appeal may also be made if the referee makes no call on a serve indicating that the serve was good. If the no call is reversed, it will result in second serve if the infraction occurred on the first serve or loss of serve if the infraction occurred on the second serve.

(c) Out Serve. If the referee makes a call of out serve, the call may be appealed. If the call is reversed, the serve will be replayed, unless the serve was obviously a fault in which case the call becomes fault serve. However, when the call is reversed and the serve is considered an ace, a point will be awarded. An appeal may also be made if the referee makes no call on a serve (indicating that the serve was good.) If the no call is reversed, it results in an immediate loss of serve.

(d) Double Bounce Pickup. If the referee makes a call of two bounces, the call may be appealed. If the call is reversed, the rally is replayed, except if the player against whom the call was made hit a shot that could not have been retrieved, then that player wins the rally. (Before awarding a rally in that situation, the referee must be certain that the shot would not have been retrieved even if play had not been halted.) An appeal may also be made if the referee makes no call thereby indicating that the get was not two bounces. If the no call is reversed, the player who made the two bounce pickup is declared the loser of the rally.

(e) Receiving Line Violation (Encroachment). If the referee makes a call of encroachment, the call may be appealed. If the call is overturned, the service shall be replayed. An appeal may also be made if the referee makes no call. If the appeal is successful, the server is awarded a point.

(f) Court Hinder. If the referee makes a call of court hinder, the rally is replayed. If the referee makes no call and a player feels that a court hinder occurred, that player may appeal. If the appeal is successful, the rally will be replayed.

Rule 3.9 Rules Interpretations

If a player feels the referee has interpreted the rules incorrectly, the player may require the referee or tournament director to show him the applicable rule in the rulebook. Having discovered a misapplication or misinterpretation, the official must correct the error by replaying the rally, awarding the point, calling sideout or taking whatever corrective measure necessary.

4—Play Regulations

Rule 4.1 Serve

The player or team winning the coin toss has the option to either serve or receive at the start of the first game. The second game will begin in reverse order of the first game. The player or team scoring the highest total of points in games 1 and 2 will have the option to serve or receive first at the start of the tiebreaker. In the event that both players or teams score an equal number of points in the first two games, another coin toss will take place and the winner of the toss will have the option to serve or receive.

Rule 4.2 Start

The server may not start the service motion until the referee has called the score or "second serve." When there is no referee, the server makes the call. The serve is started from any place within the service zone. Certain drive serves are an exception, see Rule 4.6. Neither the ball, nor any part of either foot may extend beyond either line of the service zone when initiating the service motion. Stepping on, but not over, the lines is permitted. When completing the service motion, the server may step over the service (front) line provided that some part of both feet remain on or inside the line until the served ball passes the short line. The server may not step over the short line until the ball passes the short line. See Rules 4.10 (a) and 4.11 (k) for penalties for violations.

Rule 4.3 Manner

After taking a set position inside the service zone, a player may begin the service motion—any continuous movement which results in the ball being served. Once the service motion begins, the ball must be bounced on the floor in the zone and be struck by the racquet before it bounces a second time. After being struck, the ball must hit the front wall first and on the rebound hit the floor beyond the back edge of the short line, either with or without touching one of the side walls.

Rule 4.4 Readiness

The service motion shall not begin until the referee has called the score or the second serve and the server has visually checked the receiver. The referee shall call the score as both server and receiver prepare to return to their respective positions, shortly after the previous rally has ended.

Rule 4.5 Delays

Except as noted in Rule 4.5 (b), delays exceeding 10 seconds shall result in an out if the server is the offender or a point if the receiver is the offender.

(a) The 10 second rule is applicable to the server and receiver simultaneously. Collectively, they are allowed up to 10 seconds, after the score is called, to serve or be ready to receive. It is the server's responsibility to look and be certain the receiver is ready. If the receiver is not ready, he must signal so by raising his racquet above his head or completely turning his back to the server. (These are the only two acceptable signals.)

(b) Serving while the receiving player/team is signalling not ready is a fault serve.

(c) After the score is called, if the server looks at the receiver and the receiver is not signalling not ready, the server may then serve. If the receiver attempts to signal not ready after that point, the signal shall not be acknowledged and the serve becomes legal.

Rule 4.6 Drive Service Zones

The drive serve lines will be 3 feet from each side wall in the service box, dividing the service area in two 17-foot service zones for drive serves only. The player may drive serve between himself and the side wall nearest to where his service motion began only if the player starts and remains outside of the 3-foot drive service zone. In the event that the service motion begins in one drive service zone and continues into the other drive serve zone, the player may not hit a drive serve at all. Violations of this rule, either called or not called, may be appealed.

(a) The drive serve zones are not observed for crosscourt drive serves, the hard-Z, soft-Z, lob or half-lob serves.

(b) The racquet may not break the plane of the 17-foot zone while making contact with the ball.

(c) The drive serve line is not part of the 17-foot zone. Dropping the ball on the line or standing on the line while serving to the same side is an infraction.

Rule 4.7 Serve in Doubles

(a) Order of Serve. Each team shall inform the referee of the order of service which shall be followed throughout that game. The order of serve may be changed between games. At the beginning of each game, when the first server of the first team to serve is out, the team is out. Thereafter, both players on each team shall serve until the team receives a handout and a sideout.

(b) Partner's Position. On each serve, the server's partner shall stand erect with back to the side wall and with both feet on the floor within the service box from the moment the server begins the service motion until the served ball passes the short line. Violations are called foot faults. However, if the server's partner enters the safety zone before the ball passes the short line, the server loses service.

Rule 4.8 Defective Serves

Defective serves are of three types resulting in penalties as follows:

(a) Dead-Ball Serve. A dead-ball serve results in no penalty and the server is given another serve (without canceling a prior fault serve).

(b) Fault Serve. Two fault serves result in an out (either a sideout or a handout).

(c) Out Serve. An out serve results in an out (either a sideout or a handout.)

Rule 4.9 Dead-Ball Serves

Dead-ball serves do not cancel any previous fault serve. The following are dead-ball serves:

(a) Ball Hits Partner. A serve which strikes the server's partner while in the doubles box is a dead-ball serve. A serve which touches the floor before touching the server's partner is a short serve.

(b) Court Hinders. A serve that takes an irregular bounce because it hit a wet spot or an irregular surface on the court is a dead-ball serve. Also, any serve that hits any surface designated by local rules as an obstruction.

(c) Broken Ball. If the ball is determined to have broken on the serve, a new ball shall be substituted and the serve shall be replayed, not canceling any prior fault serve.

Rule 4.10 Fault Serves

The following serves are faults and any two in succession result in an out:

(a) Foot Faults. A foot fault results when:
   1. The server does not begin the service motion with both feet in the service zone.

2. The server steps completely over the service line (no part of the foot on or inside the service zone) before the served ball crosses the short line.
3. In doubles, the server's partner is not in the service box with both feet on the floor and back to the side wall from the time the server begins the service motion until the ball passes the short line. See Rule 4.7 (b).

(b) Short Service. A short serve is any served ball that first hits the front wall and, on the rebound, hits the floor on or in front of the short line either with or without touching a side wall.

(c) Three-Wall Serve. A three-wall serve is any served ball that first hits the front wall and, on the rebound, strikes both side walls before touching the floor.

(d) Ceiling Serve. A ceiling serve is any served ball that first hits the front wall and then touches the ceiling (with or without touching a side wall).

(e) Long Serve. A long serve is a served ball that first hits the front wall and rebounds to the back wall before touching the floor (with or without touching a side wall).

(f) Out-of-Court Serve. An out-of-court serve is any served ball that first hits the wall and, before striking the floor, goes out of the court.

(g) Bouncing Ball Outside Service Zone. Bouncing the ball outside the service zone as a part of the service motion is a fault serve.

(h) Illegal Drive Serve. A drive serve in which the player fails to observe the 17-foot drive service zone outlined in Rule 4.6.

(i) Screen Serve. A served ball that first hits the front wall and on the rebound passes so closely to the server, or server's partner in doubles, that it prevents the receiver from having a clear view of the ball. (The receiver is obligated to place himself in good court position, near center court, to obtain that view.) The screen serve is the only fault serve which may not be appealed.

(j) Serving before the Receiver is Ready. A serve is made while the receiver is not ready as described in Rule 4.5.

(k) Ball Hits Partner. A served ball that hits the doubles partner while in the doubles box results in a fault serve.

Rule 4.11 Out Serves

Any of the following serves results in an out:

(a) Two Consecutive Fault Serves. See Rule 4.10.

(b) Failure to Serve. Failure of server to put the ball into play under Rule 4.5.

(c) Missed Serve Attempt. Any attempt to strike the ball that results in a total miss or in the ball touching any part of the server's body. Also, allowing the ball to bounce more than once during the service motion.

(d) Touched Serve. Any served ball that on the rebound from the front wall touches the server or server's racquet, or any ball intentionally stopped or caught by the server or server's partner.

(e) Fake or Balk Serve. Any movement of the racquet toward the ball during the serve which is noncontinuous and done for the purpose of deceiving the receiver. If a balk serve occurs, but the referee believes that no deceit was involved, he has the option of declaring "no serve" and have the serve replayed without penalty.

(f) Illegal Hit. An illegal hit includes contacting the ball twice, carrying the ball, or hitting the ball with the handle of the racquet or part of the body or uniform.

(g) Non-Front Wall Serve. Any served ball that does not strike the front wall first.

(h) Crotch Serve. Any served ball that hits the crotch of the front wall and floor, front wall and side wall, or front wall and ceiling is an out serve (because it did not hit the front wall first). A serve into the crotch of the back wall and floor is a good serve and in play. A served ball that hits the crotch of the side wall and floor beyond the short line is in play.

(i) Out-of-Order Serve. In doubles, when either partner serves out of order, the points scored by that server will be subtracted and an out serve will be called: if the second server serves out of order, the out serve will be applied to the first server and the second server will resume serving. If the player designated as the first server serves out of order, a sideout will be called. The referee should call no serve as soon as an out-of-order serve occurs. If no points are scored while the team is out of order, only the out penalty will have to be assessed. However, if points are scored before the out-of-order condition is noticed and the referee cannot recall the number, the referee may enlist the aid of the line judges (if they are being used) to recall the number of points to be deducted.

(j) Ball Hits Partner. A served ball that hits the doubles partner while outside the doubles box results in loss of serve.

(k) Safety Zone Violation. If the server, or doubles partner, enters into the safety zone before the served ball passes the short line, it shall result in the loss of serve.

Rule 4.12 Return of Serve

(a) Receiving Position
   1. The receiver may not enter the safety zone until the ball bounces or crosses the receiving line.
   2. On the fly return attempt, the receiver may not strike the ball until the ball breaks the plane of the receiving line. The receiver's follow-through may carry the receiver or his racquet past the receiving line.
   3. Neither the receiver nor his racquet may break the plane of the short line, except if the ball is struck after rebounding off the back wall.
   4. Any violation by the receiver results in a point for the server.

(b) Defective Serve. A player on the receiving side may not intentionally catch or touch a served ball (such as an apparently long or short serve) until the referee has made a call or the ball has touched the floor for a second time. Violation results in a point.

(c) Legal Return. After a legal serve, a player on the receiving team must strike the ball on the fly or after the first bounce, and before the ball touches the floor the second time; and return the ball to the front wall, either directly or after touching one or both side walls, the back wall or the ceiling, or any combination of those surfaces. A returned ball must touch the front wall before touching the floor.

(d) Failure to Return. The failure to return a serve results in a point for the server.

(e) Other Provisions. Except as noted in this rule (4.12), the return of serve is subject to all provisions of Rules 4.14 through 4.16.

Rule 4.13 Changes of Serve

(a) Outs. A server is entitled to continue serving until:
  1. Out Serve. See Rule 4.11.
  2. Two Consecutive Fault Serves. See Rule 4.10.
  3. Ball Hits Partner. Player hits partner with attempted return.
  4. Failure to Return Ball. Player, or partner, fails to keep the ball in play as required by Rule 4.12 (c).
  5. Avoidable Hinder. Player or partner commits an avoidable hinder which results in an out. See Rule 4.16.
(b) Sideout. In singles, retiring the server is a sideout. In doubles, the side is retired when both partners have lost service, except that the team which serves first at the beginning of each game loses the serve when the first server is retired. See Rule 4.7.
(c) Effect of Sideout. When the server (or serving team) receives a sideout, the server becomes the receiver and the receiver becomes the server.

Rule 4.14 Rallies

All of the play which occurs after the successful return of serve is called the rally. Play shall be conducted according to the following rules:

(a) Legal Hits. Only the head of the racquet may be used at any time to return the ball. The racquet may be held in one or both hands. Switching hands to hit a ball, touching the ball with any part of the body or uniform, or removing the wrist thong results in a loss of the rally.
(b) One Touch. The player or team trying to return the ball may touch or strike the ball only once or else the rally is lost. The ball may not be carried. (A carried ball is one which rests on the racquet long enough that the effect is more of a sling or throw than a hit.)
(c) Failure to Return. Any of the following constitutes a failure to make a legal return during a rally:
  1. The ball bounces on the floor more than once before being hit.
  2. The ball does not reach the front wall on the fly.
  3. The ball caroms off a player's racquet into a gallery or wall opening without first hitting the front wall.
  4. A ball which obviously does not have the velocity or direction to hit the front wall strikes another player.
  5. A ball struck by one player on a team hits the player or that player's partner.
  6. Committing an avoidable hinder. See Rule 4.16.
  7. Switching hands during a rally.
  8. Failure to use wrist thong on racquet.
  9. Touching the ball with the body or uniform.
  10. Carry or sling the ball with the racquet.
(d) Effect of Failure to Return. Violations of Rules 4.14 (a) through (c) result in a loss of rally. If the serving player or team loses the rally, it is an out. If the receiver loses the rally, it results in a point for the server.

(e) Return Attempts. The ball remains in play until it touches the floor a second time, regardless of how many walls it makes contact with—including the front wall.
   1. In singles, if a player swings at the ball and misses it, the player may continue to attempt to return the ball until it touches the floor for the second time.
   2. In doubles, if one player swings at the ball and misses it, both partners may make further attempts to return the ball until it touches the floor the second time. Both partners on a side are entitled to return the ball.
(f) Out-of-Court Ball
   1. After return. Any ball returned to the front wall which, on the rebound or the first bounce, goes into the gallery or through any opening in a side wall shall be declared dead and the server shall receive two serves.
   2. No Return. Any ball not returned to the front wall, but which caroms off a player's racquet into the gallery or into any opening in a side wall either with or without touching the ceiling, side wall, or back wall, shall be an out for the player failing to make the return, or a point for the opponent.
(g) Broken Ball. If there is any suspicion that a ball has broken during a rally, play shall continue until the end of the rally. The referee or any player may request the ball be examined. If the referee decides the ball is broken the ball will be replaced and the rally replayed. The server will get two serves. The only proper way to check for a broken ball is to squeeze it by hand. (Checking the ball by striking it with a racquet will not be considered a valid check and shall work to the disadvantage of the player or team which struck the ball after the rally.)
(h) Play Stoppage
   1. If a foreign object enters the court, or any other outside interference occurs, the referee shall stop the play immediately and declare a dead-ball hinder.
   2. If a player loses any apparel, or equipment, or other article, the referee shall stop play immediately and declare an avoidable hinder or dead-ball hinder as described in Rule 4.16 (i).
(i) Replays. Whenever a rally is replayed for any reason, the server is awarded two serves. A previous fault serve is not considered.

Rule 4.15 Dead-Ball Hinders

A rally is replayed without penalty and the server receives two serves whenever a dead-ball hinder occurs.

(a) Situations
   1. Court Hinders. The referee should stop play immediately whenever the ball hits any part of the court that was designated in advance as a court hinder (such as a door handle). The referee should also stop play (i) when the ball takes an irregular bounce as a result of contacting a rough surface (such as court light or vent) or after striking a wet spot on the floor or wall and (ii) when, in the referee's opinion, the irregular bounce affected the rally. A court hinder is the only type of hinder that is appealable. See Rule 3.7 (a).

2. Ball Hits Opponent. When an opponent is hit by a return shot in flight, it is a dead-ball hinder. If the opponent is struck by a ball which obviously did not have the velocity or direction to reach the front wall, it is not a hinder, and the player who hit the ball will lose the rally. A player who has been hit by the ball can stop play and make the call though the call must be made immediately and acknowledged by the referee.

3. Body Contact. If body contact occurs which the referee believes was sufficient to stop the rally, either for the purpose of preventing injury by further contact or because the contact prevented a player from being able to make a reasonable return, the referee shall call a hinder. Incidental body contact in which the offensive player clearly will have the advantage should not be called a hinder, unless the offensive player obviously stops play. Contact with the racquet on the follow-through normally is not considered a hinder.

4. Screen Ball. Any ball rebounding from the front wall so close to the body of the defensive team that it interferes with, or prevents, the offensive player from having clear view of the ball. The referee should be careful not to make the screen call so quickly that it takes away a good offensive opportunity. A ball that passes between the legs of the side that just returned the ball is not automatically a screen. It depends on the proximity of the players. Again, the call should work to the advantage of the offensive player.

5. Backswing Hinder. Any body or racquet contact, on the backswing or on the way to or just prior to returning the ball, which impairs the hitter's ability to take a reasonable swing. This call can be made by the player attempting the return, though the call must be made immediately and is subject to the referee's approval. Note the interference may be considered an avoidable hinder. See Rule 4.16.

6. Safety Holdup. Any player about to execute a return who believes he is likely to strike his opponent with the ball or racquet may immediately stop play and request a dead-ball hinder. This call must be made immediately and is subject to acceptance and approval of the referee. (The referee will grant a dead-ball hinder if it is believed the holdup was reasonable and the player would have been able to return the shot, and the referee may also call an avoidable hinder if warranted.)

7. Other Interference. Any other unintentional interference which prevents an opponent from having a fair chance to see or return the ball. Example: When a ball from another court enters the court during a rally or when a referee's call on an adjacent court obviously distracts a player.

(b) Effect of Hinders. The referee's call of hinder stops play and voids any situation which follows, such as the ball hitting the player. The only hinders that may be called by a player are described in rules (2), (5), and (6) above, and all of these are subject to the approval of the referee. A dead-ball hinder stops play and the rally is replayed. The server receives two serves.

(c) Avoidance. While making an attempt to return the ball, a player is entitled to a fair chance to see and return the ball. It is the responsibility of the side that has just hit the ball to move so the receiving side may go straight to the ball and have an unobstructed view of the ball. In the judgment of the referee however, the receiver must make a reasonable effort to move towards the ball and have a reasonable chance to return the ball in order for a hinder to be called.

Rule 4.16 Avoidable Hinders

An avoidable hinder results in the loss of the rally. An avoidable hinder does not necessarily have to be an intentional act and is the result of any of the following:

(a) Failure to Move. A player does not move sufficiently to allow an opponent a shot straight to the front wall as well as a crosscourt shot which is a shot directly to the front wall at an angle that would cause the ball to rebound directly to the rear corner farthest from the player hitting the ball. Also when a player moves in such a direction that it prevents an opponent from taking either of these shots.

(b) Stroke Interference. This occurs when a player moves, or fails to move, so that the opponent returning the ball does not have a free, unimpeded swing. This includes unintentionally moving the wrong direction which prevents an opponent from making an open offensive shot.

(c) Blocking. Moves into a position which blocks the opponent from getting to, or returning, the ball; or in doubles, a player moves in front of an opponent as the player's partner is returning the ball.

(d) Moving into the Ball. Moves in the way and is struck by the ball just played by the opponent.

(e) Pushing. Deliberately pushes or shoves opponent during a rally.

(f) Intentional Distractions. Deliberate shouting, stamping of feet, waving of racquet, or any other manner of disrupting one's opponent.

(g) View Obstruction. A player moves across an opponent's line of vision just before the opponent strikes the ball.

(h) Wetting the Ball. The players, particularly the server, should insure that the ball is dry prior to the serve. Any wet ball that is not corrected prior to the serve shall result in an avoidable hinder against the server.

(i) Apparel or Equipment Loss. If a player loses any apparel, equipment, or other article, play shall be immediately stopped and that player shall be called for an avoidable hinder, unless the player has just hit a shot that could not be retrieved. If the loss of equipment is caused by a player's opponent, then a dead-ball hinder should be called. If the opponent's action is judged to have been avoidable, then the opponent should be called for an avoidable hinder.

Rule 4.17 Timeouts

(a) Rest Periods. Each player or team is entitled to three 30-second timeouts in games to 15 and two 30-second timeouts in games to 11. Timeouts may not be called by either side after service motion has begun. Calling for a timeout when none remain or after service motion has begun, or taking more than 30 seconds in a timeout, will result in the assessment of a technical foul for delay of game.

(b) Injury. If a player is injured during the course of a match as a result of contact, such as with the ball, racquet, wall or floor, he will be awarded an injury timeout. While a player may call more than one timeout for the same injury or for additional injuries which occur during the match, a player is not allowed more than a total of 15 minutes of rest during a match. If the injured player is not able to resume play after total rest of 15 minutes, the match shall be awarded to the opponent. Muscle cramps and pulls, fatigue, and other ailments that are not caused by direct contact on the court will not be considered an injury.

(c) Equipment Timeouts. Players are expected to keep all clothing and equipment in good, playable condition and are expected to use regular timeouts and time between games for adjustment and replacement of equipment. If a player or team is out of timeouts and the referee determines that an equipment change or adjustment is necessary for fair and safe continuation of the match, the referee may award an equipment timeout not to exceed 2 minutes. The referee may allow additional time under unusual circumstances.

(d) Between Games. The rest period between the first two games of a match is 2 minutes. If a tiebreaker is necessary, the rest period between the second and third game is 5 minutes.

(e) Postponed Games. Any games postponed by referees shall be resumed with the same score as when postponed.

Rule 4.18 Technical Fouls and Warnings

(a) Technical Fouls. The referee is empowered to deduct one point from a player's or team's score when, in the referee's sole judgment, the player is being overtly and deliberately abusive. If the player or team against whom the technical foul was assessed does not resume play immediately, the referee is empowered to forfeit the match in favor of the opponent. Some examples of actions which may result in technical fouls are:
1. Profanity.
2. Excessive arguing.
3. Threat of any nature to opponent or referee.
4. Excessive or hard striking of the ball between rallies.
5. Slamming of the racquet against walls or floor, slamming the door, or any action which might result in injury to the court or other players.
6. Delay of game. Examples include (i) taking too much time to dry the court, (ii) questioning of the referee excessively about the rules, (iii) exceeding the time allotted for timeouts or between games, or (iv) calling a timeout when none remain.
7. Intentional front line foot fault to negate a bad lob serve.
8. Anything considered to be unsportsmanlike behavior.
9. Failure to wear lensed eyewear designed for racquet sports is an automatic technical foul on the first infraction and a mandatory timeout will be charged against the offending player to acquire the proper eyewear. A second infraction by that player during the match will result in automatic forfeiture of the match.

(b) Technical Warnings. If a player's behavior is not so severe as to warrant a technical foul, a technical warning may be issued without point deduction.

(c) Effect of Technical Foul or Warning. If a referee issues a technical foul, one point shall be removed from the offender's score. If a referee issues a technical warning, it shall not result in a loss of rally or point and shall be accompanied by a brief explanation of the reason for the warning. The issuing of the technical foul or warning has no effect on who will be serving when play resumes. If a technical foul occurs between games or when the offender has no points, the result will be that the offender's score will revert to minus one (–1).

5—Tournaments

Rule 5.1 Draws

(a) If possible, all draws shall be made at least 2 days before the tournament commences. The seeding method of drawing shall be approved by the AARA.

(b) At AARA National events, the draw and seeding committee shall be chaired by the AARA's Executive Director, National Tournament Director, and the host tournament director. No other persons shall participate in the draw or seeding unless at the invitation of the draw and seeding committee.

(c) In local and regional tournaments, the draw shall be the responsibility of the tournament director.

Rule 5.2 Scheduling

(a) Preliminary Matches. If one or more contestants are entered in both singles and doubles, they may be required to play both singles and doubles on the same day or night with little rest between matches. This is a risk assumed on entering two singles events or a singles and doubles event. If possible, the schedule should provide at least 1 hour between matches.

(b) Final Matches. Where one or more players has reached the finals in both singles and doubles, it is recommended that the doubles match be played on the day preceding the singles. This would assure more rest between the final matches. If both final matches must be played on the same day or night, the following procedure is recommended that:
1. The singles match be played first and
2. A rest period of not less than 1 hour be allowed between the finals in singles and doubles.

Rule 5.3 Notice of Matches

After the first round of matches, it is the responsibility of each player to check the posted schedules to determine the time and place of each subsequent match. If any change is made in the schedule after posting, it shall be the duty of the committee or tournament director to notify the players of the change.

Rule 5.4 Third Place

Players are not required to play off for 3rd place. However, for point standings, if one semifinalist wants to play off for third and the other semifinalist does not, the one willing to play shall be awarded third place. If neither semifinalist wishes to play off for 3rd then the points shall be totaled, divided by 2, and awarded evenly to both players.

Rule 5.5 Round Robin Scoring

The final positions of players or teams in round robin competition is determined by the following sequence:

(a) Winner of the most matches;
(b) In a two-way tie, winner of the head-to-head match;
(c) In a tie of three or more, the player who lost the fewest games is awarded the highest position.
    1. If a two-way tie remains, the winner of the head-to-head match is awarded the higher position.
    2. If a multiple tie remains, the total points scored against each player in all matches will be tabulated and the player who had the least points scored against him is awarded the highest position. Note: Forfeits will count as a match won in two games. In cases where points scored against is the tiebreaker, the points scored by the forfeiting team will be discounted from consideration of points scored against all teams.

Rule 5.6 Tournament Management

In all AARA sanctioned tournaments, the tournament director and/or AARA official in attendance may decide on a change of court after the completion of any tournament game, if such a change will accommodate better spectator conditions.

Rule 5.7 Tournament Conduct

In all AARA sanctioned tournaments, the referee is empowered to forfeit a match, if the conduct of a player or team is considered detrimental to the tournament and the game. See Rules 3.5 (d) and (e).

Rule 5.8 Professional

A professional is defined as any player who has accepted prize money regardless of the amount in any professional sanctioned (including WPRA and IRT) tournament or in any other tournament so deemed by the AARA Board of Directors. (Note: Any player concerned about the adverse effect of losing amateur status should contact the AARA National Office at the earliest opportunity to ensure a clear understanding of this rule and that no action is taken that could jeopardize that status.)

(a) An amateur player may participate in a professional sanctioned tournament but will not be considered a professional (i) if no prize money is accepted or (ii) if the prize money received remains intact and placed in trust under AARA guidelines.

(b) The acceptance of merchandise or travel expenses shall not be considered prize money, and thus does not jeopardize a player's amateur status.

Rule 5.9 Return to Amateur Status

Any player who has been classified as a professional can recover amateur status by requesting, in writing, this desire to be reclassified as an amateur. This application shall be tendered to the Executive Director of the AARA or his designated representative, and shall become effective immediately as long as the player making application for reinstatement of amateur status has received no money in any tournament, as defined in Rule 5.8 for the past 12 months.

Rule 5.10 AARA Eligibility

(a) Any current AARA member who has not been classified as a professional (see Rule 5.8) may compete in any AARA sanctioned tournament.
(b) Any current AARA member who has been classified as a professional may compete in any event at an AARA sanctioned tournament that offers prize money or merchandise.

Rule 5.11 Divisions

(a) Open Division. Any player with amateur status.
(b) Adult Age Divisions. Eligibility is determined by the player's age on the first day of the tournament. Divisions are:

19+	Junior Veterans	55+	Golden Masters
25+	Junior Veterans	60+	Veteran Golden Masters
30+	Veterans	65+	Senior Golden Masters
35+	Seniors	70+	Advanced Golden Masters
40+	Veteran Seniors	75+	Super Golden Masters
45+	Masters	80+	Grand Masters
50+	Veteran Masters		

(c) Junior Age Divisions. Player eligibility is determined by the player's age on January 1st of the current calendar year. Divisions are:

18 & Under	10 & Under
16 & Under	8 & Under
14 & Under	8 & Under Multi-Bounce
12 & Under	

Rule 5.12 Division Competition by Gender

Men and women may compete only in events and divisions for their respective gender during regional and national tournaments. If there is not sufficient number of players to warrant play in a specific division, the tournament director may place the entrants in a comparably competitive division. Note: For the purpose of encouraging the development of women's racquetball, the governing bodies of numerous states permit women to play in men's divisions when a comparable skill level is not available in the women's divisions.

Rule 5.13 AARA Regional Championships

(a) Adult Regional Tournaments
1. Regional tournaments will be conducted at various metro sites designated annually by the AARA and players may compete at any site they choose.
2. A person may compete in any number of adult regional tournaments, but may not enter a championship (no skill designation) division after having won that division at a previous adult regional tournament that same year.
3. A person cannot participate in more than two championship events at a regional tournament.
4. Any awards or remuneration to an AARA National Championship will be posted on the entry blank.
(b) Junior Regional Tournaments. All provisions of Rule 5.13 (a) also apply to juniors, except:
1. Regional tournaments will be conducted within the following regions which are identified for the purposes of junior competition:

Region 1	Maine, New Hampshire, Vermont, Massachusetts, Rhode Island, Connecticut
Region 2	New York, New Jersey
Region 3	Pennsylvania, Maryland, Virginia, Delaware, District of Columbia
Region 4	Florida, Georgia
Region 5	Alabama, Mississippi, Tennessee
Region 6	Arkansas, Kansas, Missouri, Oklahoma
Region 7	Texas, Louisiana
Region 8	Wisconsin, Iowa, Illinois
Region 9	West Virginia, Ohio, Michigan
Region 10	Indiana, Kentucky
Region 11	North Dakota, South Dakota, Minnesota, Nebraska
Region 12	Arizona, New Mexico, Utah, Colorado
Region 13	Montana, Wyoming
Region 14	California, Hawaii, Nevada
Region 15	Washington, Idaho, Oregon, Alaska
Region 16	North Carolina, South Carolina

2. A person may compete in only one junior regional singles and one junior regional doubles tournament each year.
3. Rule 5.13 (a)(3) may not apply if tournaments (singles/doubles or adults/juniors) are combined.

Rule 5.14 U.S. National Singles and Doubles Championships

The U.S. National Singles and Doubles Tournaments are separate tournaments and are played on different dates. Consolation events will be offered for all divisions.

(a) Competition in an adult regional singles tournament is required to qualify for the National Singles Championship. Current National Champions are exempt from qualifying for the next year's championships.

(b) The National Tournament Director may handle the rating of each region and determine how many players shall qualify from each regional tournament.

(c) If a region is over subscribed, a playoff to qualify players in a division may be conducted the day prior to the start of a National Championship.

Rule 5.15 U.S. National Junior Olympic Championships

It will be conducted on a different date than all other National Championships and generally subject to the provisions of Rule 5.14.

Rule 5.16 U.S. National Intercollegiate Championships

It will be conducted on a different date than all other National Championships. Consolation events will be offered for all divisions.

Rule 5.17 U.S. National Skill Level (A,B,C,D) Championships

6—Eight and Under Multi-Bounce Modifications

In general, the AARA's standard rules governing racquetball play will be followed except for the modifications which follow.

Rule 6.1 Basic Return Rule

In general, the ball remains in play as long as it is bouncing. However, the player may swing only once at the ball and the ball is considered dead at the point it stops bouncing and begins to roll. Also, anytime the ball rebounds off the back wall, it must be struck before it crosses the short line on the way to the front wall, except as explained in Rule 6.2.

Rule 6.2 Blast Rule

If the ball caroms from the front wall to the back wall on the fly, the player may hit the ball from any place on the court—including past the short line—as long as the ball is bouncing.

Rule 6.3 Front Wall Lines

Two parallel lines (tape may be used) should be placed across the front wall such that the bottom edge of one line is 3 feet above the floor and the bottom edge of the other line is 1 foot above the floor. During the rally, any ball that hits the front wall (i) below the 3-foot line and (ii) either on or above the 1-foot line must be returned before it bounces a third time. However, if the ball hits below the 1-foot line, it must be returned before it bounces twice. If the ball hits on or above the 3-foot line, the ball must be returned as described in the basic return rule.

Rule 6.4 Games and Matches

All games are played to 11 points and the first side to win two games, wins the match.

7—One-Wall and Three-Wall Modifications

In general, the AARA's standard rules governing racquetball play will be followed except for the modifications which follow.

Rule 7.1 One-Wall

There are two playing surfaces, the front wall and the floor. The wall is 20 feet wide and 16 feet high. The floor is 20 feet wide and 34 feet to the back edge of the long line. To permit movement by players, there should be a minimum of three feet (six feet is recommended) beyond the long line and six feet outside each side line.

(a) Short Line. The back edge of the short line is 16 feet from the wall.
(b) Service Markers. Lines at least six inches long which are parallel with, and midway between, the long and short lines. The extension of the service markers form the imaginary boundary of the service line.
(c) Service Zone. The entire floor area inside and including the short line, sidelines and service line.
(d) Receiving Zone. The entire floor area in back of the short line, including the sidelines and the long line.

Rule 7.2 Three-Wall with Short Sidewall

The front wall is 20 feet wide and 20 feet high. The side walls are 20 feet long and 20 feet high, with the sidewalls tapering to 12 feet high. The floor length and court markings are the same as a four-wall court.

Rule 7.3 Three-Wall with Long Sidewall

The court is 20 feet wide, 20 feet high and 40 feet long. The sidewalls may taper from 20 feet high at the front wall down to 12 feet high at the end of the court. All court markings are the same as a four-wall court.

Rule 7.4 Service in Three-Wall Courts

A serve that goes beyond the sidewalls on the fly is an out. A serve that goes beyond the long line on a fly, but within the sidewalls, is a fault.

8—Wheelchair Modifications

Rule 8.1 Changes to Standard Rules

In general, the AARA's standard rules governing racquetball play will be followed except for the modifications which follow.

(a) Where AARA rules refer to server, person, body, or other similar variations, for wheelchair play such reference shall include all parts of the wheelchair in addition to the person sitting on it.

(b) Where the rules refer to feet, standing or other similar descriptions, for wheelchair play it means only where the rear wheels actually touch the floor.

(c) Where the rules mention body contact, for wheelchair play it shall mean any part of the wheelchair in addition to the player.

(d) Where the rules refer to double bounce or after the first bounce, it shall mean three bounces. All variations of the same phrases shall be revised accordingly.

Rule 8.2 Divisions

(a) Novice Division. The Novice Division is for the beginning player who is just learning to play.

(b) Intermediate Division. The Intermediate Division is for the player who has played tournaments before and has a skill level to be competitive in the division.

(c) Open Division. The Open Division is the highest level of play and is for the advanced player.

(d) Multi-Bounce Division. The Multi-Bounce Division is for the individuals (men or women) whose mobility is such that wheelchair racquetball would be impossible if not for the Multi-Bounce Division.

(e) Junior Division. The junior divisions are for players who are under the age of 19. The tournament director will determine if the divisions will be played as two bounce or multi-bounce. Age divisions are: 8–11, 12–15, and 16–18.

Rule 8.3 Rules

(a) Two Bounce Rule. Two bounces are used in wheelchair racquetball in all divisions except the Multi-Bounce Division. The ball may hit the floor twice before being returned.

(b) Out-of-Chair Rule. The player can neither intentionally jump out of his chair to hit a ball nor stand up in his chair to serve the ball. If the referee determines that the chair was left intentionally it will result in loss of the rally for the offender. If a player unintentionally leaves his chair, no penalty will be assessed. Repeat offenders will be warned by the referee.

(c) Equipment Standards. In order to protect playing surfaces, the tournament officials may not allow a person to participate with black tires or anything which will mark or damage the court.

(d) Start. The serve may be started from any place within the service zone. Although the front casters may extend beyond the lines of the service zone, at no time shall the rear wheels cross either the service or short line before the served ball crosses the short line. Penalties for violation are the same as those for the standard game.

(e) Maintenance Delay. A maintenance delay is a delay in the progress of a match due to a malfunction of a wheelchair, prosthesis, or assistive device. Such delay must be requested by the player, granted by the referee during the match, and shall not exceed 5 minutes. Only two such delays may be granted for each player for each match. After using both maintenance delays, the player has the following options:
1. Continue play with the defective equipment.
2. Immediately substitute replacement equipment.
3. Postpone the game, with the approval of the referee and opponent.

Rule 8.4 Multi-Bounce Rules

(a) The ball may bounce as many times as the receiver wants though the player may. swing only once to return the ball to the front wall.

(b) The ball must be hit before it crosses the short line on its way back to the front wall.

(c) The receiver cannot cross the short line after the ball contacts the back wall.

9—Visually Impaired Modifications

In general, the AARA's standard rules governing racquetball play will be followed except for the modifications which follow.

Rule 9.1 Eligibility

A player's visual acuity must not be better than 20/200 with the best practical eye correction or else the player's field of vision must not be better than 20 degrees. The three classifications of blindness are B1 (totally blind to light perception), B2 (able to see hand movement up to 20/600 corrected), and B3 (from 20/600 to 20/200 corrected).

Rule 9.2 Return of Serve and Rallies

On the return of serve and on every return thereafter, the player may make multiple attempts to strike the ball until (i) the ball has been touched, (ii) the ball has stopped bouncing, or (iii) the ball has passed the short line after touching the back wall. The only exception is described in Rule 8.3.

Rule 9.3 Blast Rule

If the ball (other than on the serve) caroms from the front wall to the back wall on the fly, the player may retrieve the ball from any place on the court—including in front of the short line—as long as the ball has not been touched and is still bouncing.

Rule 9.4 Hinders

A dead-ball hinder will result in the rally being replayed without penalty unless the hinder was intentional. If a hinder is clearly intentional, an avoidable hinder should be called and the rally awarded to the nonoffending player or team.

10—National Racquetball Association of the Deaf [NRAD] Modifications

In general, the AARA's standard rules governing racquetball play will be followed except for the modifications which follow.

Rule 10.1 Eligibility

An athlete shall have a hearing loss of 55 db or more in the better ear to be eligible for any NRAD tournament.

11—Women's Professional Racquetball Association [WPRA] Modifications

In general, the AARA's standard rules governing racquetball play will be followed for competition on the Women's Professional Racquetball Association tour, except for the modifications which follow.

Rule 11.1 Match, Game, Super Tiebreaker

A match is won by the first side winning three games. All games, other than the fifth one, are won by the first side to score 11 points. The fifth game, called the super tiebreaker, is won by the first side scoring 11 points and having at least a 2-point lead. If necessary, the game will continue beyond 11 points until such time as one side has a 2-point lead.

Rule 11.2 Appeals

There is no limit on the number of appeals that a player or team may make.

Rule 11.3 Serve

The server may leave the service zone as soon as the serve has been made.

Rule 11.4 Drive Service Zone

The server may begin a drive serve anywhere in the service zone as long as the server is completely inside the 17-foot drive service zone when the ball is actually contacted.

Rule 11.5 Return of Serve

The receiver may enter the safety zone as soon as the ball has been served. The served ball may not be contacted in the receiving zone until it has bounced. Neither the receiver nor the receiver's racquet may break the plane of the short line unless the ball is struck after rebounding off the back wall. On the fly return attempt, the receiver may not strike the ball until the ball breaks the plane of the receiving line. The receiver's follow-through may carry the receiver or the racquet past the receiving line.

Rule 11.6 Avoidable Hinder

An avoidable hinder shall be called when one of the following occurs:
(a) The player's movement or failure to move interferes with their opponent's opportunity to take an offensive shot. The player is entitled to a free, unimpeded swing on their shot. The player should not be blocked by the opponent, preventing their getting to or returning the ball for an offensive shot.
(b) Any other action or conduct described in Rules 4.16 (d) through 4.16 (i).

Rule 11.7 Timeouts

Each player or team is entitled to two 30-second timeouts per game.

Rule 11.8 Time between Games

The rest period between all games will be 2 minutes except that a 5-minute rest period will be allowed between the fourth and fifth games.

Rule 11.9 Equipment Timeouts

A player does not have to use regular timeouts to correct or adjust equipment provided that the need for the change or adjustment is acknowledged by the referee as being necessary for fair and safe continuation of the match.

12—Transcoastal International Racquetball Tour [Men's Professional] Modifications

In general, the AARA's standard rules governing racquetball play will be followed for competition in the Transcoastal International Racquetball Tour, except for the modifications which follow.

Rule 12.1 Game, Match

All games are played to 11 points, and are won by the player who scores to that level, with a 2-point lead. If necessary, the game will continue beyond 11 points, until such time as one player has a 2-point lead. Matches are played the best three out of a possible five games to 11.

Rule 12.2 Appeals

The referee's call is final. There are no line judges, and no appeals may be made.

Rule 12.3 Serve

Players are allowed only one serve to put the ball into play.

Rule 12.4 Screen Serve

Screen serves are replayed.

Rule 12.5 Court Hinders

No court hinders are allowed or called.

Rule 12.6 Out-of-Court Ball

Any ball leaving the court results in a loss of rally.

Rule 12.7 Ball

All matches are played with the Penn Pro ball.

Rule 12.8 Timeouts

Each player is entitled to one 1-minute timeout per game.

Rule 12.9 Time between Games

The rest period between all games is 2 minutes.

Rule Change Procedures

To ensure the orderly growth of racquetball, the AARA has established specific procedures that are followed before a major change is made to the rules of the game. Those procedures are:

1. Rule change proposals must be submitted in writing to the AARA National Office by June 1st.
2. The AARA Board of Directors will review all proposals at its October board meeting and determine which will be considered.
3. Selected proposals will appear in RACQUETBALL Magazine—the official AARA publication—as soon as possible after the October meeting for comment by the general membership.
4. After reviewing membership input and the recommendation of the National Rules Committee and National Rules Commissioner, the proposals are discussed and voted upon at the annual Board of Directors meeting in May.
5. Changes approved in May become effective on September 1st. Exception: changes in racquet specifications become effective 2 years later on September 1st.
6. Proposed rules that are considered for adoption in one year, but are not approved by the Board of Directors in May of that year, will not be considered for adoption the following year.

Rulebook Index

AARA National Rules Committee

Otto Dietrich, National Rules
   Commissioner
4244 Russet Court
Lilburn, GA 30247
   404/523–5950 (Office)
   404/972–2303 (Home)

Michael Arnolt
Suite 307, 3833 North Meridian Street
Indianapolis, IN 46208
   317/926–2766 (Office)
   317/259–1359 (Home)

Mickey Bellah
13402 Heritage Way, #750
Tustin, CA 92680
   714/348–0900 (Office)
   714/669–1776 (Home)

Rich Clay
3401 North Kedzie
Chicago, IL 60618
   312/539–1112 (Office)
   708/918–7407 (Home)

Mary Lyons
940 Penman Road
Neptune Beach, FL 32266
   904/268–8888 (Office)

Annie Muniz
5608 Whitehaven
Bellaire, TX 77401
   713/622–8343 (Office)
   713/723–9404 (Home)

Caryn McKinney
P.O. Box 95563
Atlanta, GA 30347
   404/636–7575 (Home)

Carlton Vass
P.O. Box 31875
Charleston, SC 29417
   803/571–7889 (Office)
   803/766–8911 (Home)

Bibliography

American Amateur Racquetball
   Association
   Official Rules of Racquetball
   1685 West Uintah
   Colorado Springs, Colorado
   80904–2921

Bloss, Margaret Varner, and Norman
   Bramall. *Squash Racquets.*
   Dubuque, Iowa: Wm. C. Brown
   Company Publishers, 1967.

Edwards, Larry R. *Racquetball.* 2nd
   Edition. Scottsdale, Arizona:
   Gorsuch Scarisbrick Publishers,
   1992.

Gurney, Walden O. "A Paddleball
   Skills Test for College Men."
   Master's thesis, Brigham Young
   University, 1966.

Kittleson, Stan. *Teaching Racquetball:
   Steps to Success.* Champaign,
   Illinois: Human Kinetics, 1993.

Marchant, William S. "Telemetered
   Cardiac Response to Participation
   in Selected Duel Sports Activities."
   Master's thesis, Brigham Young
   University, 1970.

Morgans, L., et al., "Heart Rate
   Responses During Singles and
   Doubles Competition in
   Racquetball." *The Physician and
   Sportsmedicine.* (November,
   1984). p. 64.

Peterson, Alan. "Skill Assessment for
   College Racquetball Classes."
   *Journal of Physical Education
   Recreation and Dance.* 60, no. 4,
   (April, 1989). p. 71.

Questions and Answers

True or False

1. On a serve in doubles, your teammate is allowed to be anywhere on the court. (p. 83)
2. Cutthroat is played with three players. (pp. 2, 68, 70, 74)
3. Racquetball can never be played with more than three players. (pp. 2, 68, 70, 74)
4. A "short" is an infraction of the rules which involves a penalty, and has to do with irregular serves. (pp. 71, 84)
5. A crotch ball on the serve constitutes a loss of serve. (pp. 69, 85)
6. The foot may be used to return the ball. (p. 86)
7. The receiver must stand behind the receiving line while the ball is being served. (p. 85)
8. In doubles, the server must serve from the service box. (p. 83)
9. A server may not step completely over the short line when serving. (pp. 82, 84)
10. When the serve is swung at and missed, and then lands long, it is considered a long. (p. 84)
11. A server may serve from anyplace in the service zone. (p. 81)
12. A dead ball is a ball hit with such force to "kill it" that it dies on the floor. (pp. 70, 83, 87)
13. The official rules say you can play with any type racquet. (pp. 6, 76)
14. In playing racquetball, you use the same ball as in handball. (pp. 8, 76)
15. A served ball striking the front wall, then the ceiling, before striking the floor, is a fault. (pp. 83, 84)
16. The serve may strike the sidewalls before it strikes the front wall. (p. 82)
17. The server must alternate serves from side to side. (p. 81)
18. Players on the same team must take turns hitting the ball while in play. (pp. 4, 65)
19. When a player is hindered intentionally, it is an out or a point for the hindered player. (pp. 69, 89)
20. A good backhand is not necessarily important to develop. (p. 20)
21. In racquetball, it is necessary to win by two points. (pp. 4, 74)
22. Your foot may be touching the short line on the serve. (pp. 82, 84)
23. At the beginning of a game of doubles, both team members of the first team serve the ball. (pp. 4, 83)
24. A served ball is okay if it hits behind the short line after going between the server's legs. (pp. 84, 88)
25. Two "longs" retire the server. (pp. 83, 84)
26. On the serve, the ball is allowed to strike both the front and rear walls. (p. 82)

27. A short is when the server hits the ball against both the front and rear walls. (p. 84)
28. When playing doubles, both members of a team get one serve at all times.
(pp. 4, 83)
29. Cutthroat is a game of three players where two are always against one.
(pp. 2, 68, 70, 74)
30. A receiver must play the serve on the first bounce only. (p. 85)
31. When scoring, a score of 15–14 does not decide a game, since a game must be won by a difference of 2 points. (pp. 4, 74)
32. The ball can bounce more than once before it is served. (pp. 4, 82)
33. A short is where the ball fails to hit the back wall on a serve. (p. 84)
34. Points may be scored by either server or opposition. (pp. 4, 74)
35. Opposition may not play a "short." (pp. 71, 84)
36. A serve which strikes the back wall and is designated as long may be played at the discretion of the defensive players. (p. 84)
37. Tennis balls are the official balls used in tournament racquetball. (pp. 8, 76)
38. If the ball is struck by the handle of the racquet in returning the ball, it is counted as a dead ball. (p. 86)
39. On serving, the server can hit the ball before bouncing it off the floor.
(pp. 4, 82)
40. In play, if a player makes an effort to get out of the way and there is a reasonable opportunity for the other player to get the ball, no hinder should be called. (p. 88)
41. In doubles, the partner of the server must remain in his service box area until the ball strikes the front wall. (p. 83)
42. A player who feels his view of the ball was impaired by an opponent can call "hindrance" in the absence of an official. (p. 88)
43. The hand is considered to be part of the racquet and the returned ball is still good and within play when struck by this body member. (p. 86)
44. When one player has attained a score of 15 points, he has won the game whether or not the opponent is within one point. (pp. 4, 74)
45. After one short, service is lost. (p. 84)
46. Only two players can play racquetball at one time. (pp. 2, 68, 70, 74)
47. Server must stand in left-hand side of serving box only. (p. 81)
48. We grip the racquetball racquet in the Western forehand grip. (p. 17)
49. When the ball strikes the front wall and then on the fly hits the server it is played over. (p. 84)
50. If the score is 15–14, the game ends. (pp. 4, 74)
51. If the ball hits the ceiling at any time it is an out. (p. 85)
52. The server as well as the receiver can score. (pp. 4, 74)
53. An ace is a game won by more than 11 points. (p. 69)
54. If on the serve the ball hits the server, it is a hinder and should be played over. (p. 84)
55. A kill is a serve that is so hard that your opponent cannot return it. (pp. 41, 70)
56. A three-wall serve is a legal serve. (p. 84)
57. A receiver must accept all serves. (pp. 81, 82, 84)
58. The side which is not serving the ball can score a point. (pp. 4, 74)

59. When a player is interfered with by his partner, it is not a hinder.   (pp. 70, 87, 88)
60. A hinder is any ball that can't be hit or returned.   (pp. 70, 87, 88)
61. A ball swung at but missed may still be played on.   (p. 87)
62. As long as the ball does not bounce more than once on the floor, a receiver may use any object to propel the ball to the front wall.   (p. 86)
63. If a ball breaks during play the point is replayed.   (p. 87)

Multiple Choice

1. The score should be called
   a. after both sides serve
   b. at the end of the game
   c. never
   d. before the first serve   (p. 81)
2. On the serve, the ball must
   a. be bounced first
   b. be thrown to opponent first
   c. hit the wall and pass the red line before bouncing
   d. be thrown at the corner   (pp. 4, 82)
3. A crotch ball is
   a. a ball hit that strikes the back wall and front wall successively
   b. a ball that strikes a player below the belt
   c. a ball that strikes a connection of a wall to another wall or the ceiling or floor
   d. a ball that hits the ceiling and then the wall   (pp. 69, 85)
4. A ball which is returned to the front wall and rebounds from the sidewall or front wall in such a manner that it is impossible to get is
   a. a dead ball
   b. an ace
   c. a hinder
   d. a kill   (pp. 41, 70)
5. If the server steps out of the service zone while in the act of serving, it will constitute
   a. a point for receiver
   b. a side out
   c. a foot fault
   d. a hinder   (pp. 82, 84)
6. If a player's partner is hit by a served ball while in the service box, it counts as
   a. a fault
   b. a side out
   c. a hinder
   d. a dead ball   (p. 83)
7. When a served ball hits the front wall and two sidewalls before striking the floor, it constitutes
   a. a short
   b. a side out
   c. a foot fault
   d. a three-wall serve   (p. 84)
8. A hinder is
   a. a hard serve
   b. a good player
   c. a service that completely eludes the receiver
   d. where the flight of the ball is interfered with   (pp. 70, 87, 88)
9. In doubles, if a ball is swung at, hit, but its course not altered, and the other partner makes the return, the play is ruled
   a. loss of rally
   b. successful return
   c. ace
   d. hinder   (p. 86)
10. The nonserving partner in doubles may be hit _____ times while standing in the service box during a serve, before serve is lost.
    a. 1
    b. 2
    c. 3
    d. as many times as he wants   (p. 83)

11. The choice for the right to serve shall be decided by
    a. seeing who can hit the front wall closest to the floor
    b. arm wrestling for the first serve
    c. the toss of a coin
    d. whoever wants to serve (p. 81)
12. When the ball is served, hits the front wall and then hits the crotch of the sidewall and floor, it is
    a. replayed
    b. a good serve if it isn't short
    c. a loss of serve
    d. a hinder (p. 85)
13. Before the first serve, the server calls out
    a. his score
    b. his opponent's score
    c. both scores with his first
    d. both scores with his opponent's first (p. 81)
14. Cutthroat is
    a. a game with 3 people with each player playing against the other two
    b. 5 in court
    c. 3 against 2
    d. play by yourself (pp. 2, 68, 70, 74)
15. A served ball striking the server's partner while he is still in the box is
    a. a dead ball
    b. an out
    c. a fault
    d. a hinder (p. 83)
16. If a server strikes himself with a ball on the fly which has hit the front wall, it is
    a. in play
    b. dead
    c. reserved
    d. an out-serve (p. 84)
17. There are _____ points that must be scored in racquetball.
    a. 11
    b. 15
    c. 21
    d. 18 (pp. 4, 74)
18. A _____ is a phase of play wherein there is accidental interference or obstruction of the flight of the ball not involving penalty.
    a. hinder
    b. out
    c. kill
    d. short (pp. 70, 87)
19. On the serve, the receiver must stand
    a. anywhere on the court
    b. behind the service line
    c. outside the safety zone until the ball bounces or crosses the receiving line
    d. in the service box with his back against the wall (p. 81)
20. The line running parallel with the front wall and dividing the court in half is called the
    a. service line
    b. center line
    c. short line
    d. long line (pp. 4, 5, 71, 75)
21. An infraction of the rules which involves a penalty and has to do with irregular services is called
    a. an ace
    b. a short
    c. a fault
    d. a long (pp. 70, 83)
22. If a ball hits the back wall before hitting the floor on a serve, it is
    a. a fault
    b. a dead ball
    c. a good serve
    d. a long serve (p. 84)
23. The best thing for an opponent to remember is
    a. watch his opponent
    b. watch the wall
    c. watch the ball
    d. watch his opponent's feet (p. 26)

24. Stepping over the service line or short line in the act of contacting the ball while serving would be classified as
    a. a hinder
    b. a foot fault
    c. an ace
    d. a replay (pp. 82, 84)
25. If the server fails to serve the ball legally, as specified by the rules, it
    a. is played over
    b. is a fault
    c. is a free ball
    d. is a hinder (pp. 82, 84)
26. When serving, a ball that strikes the sidewall before hitting the front wall is termed a
    a. pass
    b. hinder
    c. out serve
    d. dead ball (pp. 4, 82)
27. When the ball is dropped on a serve, it must hit no more than _____ before it is served.
    a. once
    b. twice
    c. three times
    d. four times (pp. 4, 82)
28. A serve
    a. must hit the front wall first
    b. can hit the right sidewall first
    c. can hit the left sidewall first
    d. can hit the floor or ceiling first (pp. 4, 82)
29. A dead-ball hinder is
    a. recorded as a point to the player hindered
    b. played over
    c. a loss of serve if opposition is hindered
    d. a point for offensive team (p. 87)
30. In doubles, the server's partner may leave the side box
    a. when server strikes the ball
    b. after defensive player has returned the serve
    c. after serve has crossed the short line
    d. anytime he wishes after the serve has hit the front wall (p. 83)
31. A serve which cannot be played by the defensive player is termed
    a. corner shot
    b. crotch ball
    c. smash
    d. ace (p. 69)
32. A sideout means
    a. sidewall struck first on the serve
    b. kill shot hit along sidewall
    c. retiring the server in singles
    d. all of the above (pp. 72, 74)
33. In doubles, a server's partner must
    a. stand back of the short line
    b. stand within the service box
    c. stand in the safety zone
    d. stand in left corner of court (p. 83)
34. The best position to stand in is
    a. any comfortable position
    b. one side to the front favoring the forehand
    c. one side to the front favoring the backhand
    d. in a balanced position directly facing the front (p. 15)
35. If the ball hits your hand, it is considered
    a. a dead ball
    b. an out
    c. a legitimate play
    d. a hinder (p. 86)
36. Under which circumstances must the play be repeated?
    a. an error
    b. a hinder
    c. a fault
    d. a kill (pp. 70, 87)
37. How many walls can the ball hit before the front wall on a legal service?
    a. none
    b. 1 wall
    c. 2 walls
    d. 3 walls (p. 82)

38. A "kill" is
    a. flagrant violations of rules
    b. a hinder which results in physical injury
    c. a returned ball which upon rebound totally eludes opponent
    d. a service which strikes the opponent on the fly   (pp. 41, 70)
39. A long is
    a. taking too long to hit the ball
    b. hitting the ceiling before front wall
    c. serve hitting back wall before ground
    d. serve hitting behind service zone   (p. 84)
40. How much space is between the service line and the short line?
    a. 4 feet   c. 5 feet
    b. 3 feet   d. 2 feet   (pp. 4, 69, 75)
41. What is the term for a service that can't be returned?
    a. ace   c. dead ball
    b. crotch ball   d. smash   (p. 69)
42. During play when the ball goes between a player's legs and prevents a clear
    view of the ball it is a
    a. dead ball hinder   c. crotch ball
    b. pass   d. short   (p. 88)
43. For a right-hand player, when the ball approaches you on your right side,
    which foot do you pivot with to get into position for beginning the stroke?
    a. left foot   c. neither, you meet ball face on
    b. right foot   d. none of these   (p. 17)
44. The number of walls a ball can hit on a service before striking the front wall
    and still be legal is
    a. one   c. any number
    b. two   d. none   (p. 82)

Completion

1. Explain procedure for the forehand stroke.   (p. 17)
2. Explain procedure for the backhand stroke.   (p. 20)
3. After serving the ball in singles, to what court position should you move?
   Explain why.   (p. 59)
4. What is the basic court position in doubles when playing a side-by-side
   formation?   (p. 65)
5. Describe the basic types of serves.   (p. 27)
6. Explain the "cobra" wrist position so important in racquetball.   (p. 15)
7. List three individual drills that can speed up progress in racquetball.   (p. 52)

Question Answer Key

True or False

1. F	14. F	27. F	40. T	53. F
2. T	15. T	28. F	41. F	54. F
3. F	16. F	29. T	42. T	55. F
4. T	17. F	30. F	43. F	56. F
5. T	18. F	31. F	44. T	57. F
6. F	19. T	32. F	45. F	58. F
7. T	20. F	33. F	46. F	59. T
8. F	21. F	34. F	47. F	60. F
9. T	22. T	35. T	48. F	61. T
10. T	23. F	36. F	49. F	62. F
11. F	24. F	37. F	50. T	63. T
12. F	25. T	38. F	51. F	
13. F	26. F	39. F	52. F	

Multiple Choice

1. d	10. d	19. c	28. a	37. a
2. a	11. c	20. c	29. b	38. c
3. c	12. b	21. c	30. c	39. c
4. d	13. c	22. d	31. d	40. c
5. c	14. a	23. c	32. c	41. a
6. d	15. a	24. b	33. b	42. a
7. d	16. d	25. b	34. d	43. b
8. d	17. b	26. c	35. b	44. d
9. a	18. a	27. a	36. b	

Completion

1. a. Grip. Stand the edge of racquet frame on a table and shake hands with the handle so that the V formed by the thumb and index finger is directly on top of racquet handle.
   b. Stance. Left shoulder will point toward the front wall and the right shoulder toward the back wall. Weight on the balls of the feet and the knees slightly bent.
   c. Backswing. Draw arm back with the wrist fully cocked and the racquet at approximately head height. The arm is bent at approximately a 90-degree angle.
   d. Forward swing. Shift body weight from right to left with the knees bent. As you stride into the ball, dip the hitting shoulder to help lower the racquet. The wrist remains in a cocked position and the arm is bent and tucked in close to the side of the body.
   e. Impact. Contact is made off from the front foot. Just before impact, snap the wrist forward so that the racquet face is vertical and traveling in a straight line into the ball. Keep good visual contact with the ball and let the ball drop as low as possible before impact.

f. Follow-through. As the wrist is snapped through the ball, the left arm moves out of the way to pull the body through the final part of stroke. Body remains low with bent legs, until stroke is completed. Racquet continues up behind left side of the head. Return to ready position as soon as possible for the next shot.

2. a. Grip. Hand is placed on the racquet handle so that the V formed by the thumb and index finger is directly on top of the left diagonal of the handle.

   b. Stance. Right shoulder will point toward the front wall and the left shoulder toward the back wall. Weight on the balls of the feet and the knees slightly bent.

   c. Backswing. Pull racquet back with the wrist cocked, and the racquet head up and in line with the forearm. Arm is bent at the elbow and the knees are bent, with the shoulders rotated, so that racquet is approximately head high.

   d. Forward swing. Step forward and shift weight to the front leg. Rotate shoulders and pivot hips into the shot, hitting arm starts to extend but racquet is still back with the wrist in a cocked position.

   e. Impact. Just before impact, the hitting arm is nearly extended and the wrist starts to snap as the shoulder pulls the racquet through the stroke. Contact with ball is made off the front foot; at the moment of impact, the hitting arm is fully extended and the wrist snaps through the ball. Don't allow wrist to roll over at impact, and maintain good eye contact.

   f. Follow-through. Allow racquet to follow through to right side of body. Keep wrist firm and the racquet horizontal to give maximum direction to ball. Hitting shoulder is pulled through and play returns to ready position for next shot.

3. Move to area just behind the back service line that is about 9 feet from the back wall and to within 2 to 3 feet of both sidewalls. This allows you to control the center court area so that most shots hit by your opponent that strike a sidewall will angle toward this area and allow you to return the shot.

4. Each player has the responsibility for one half of the court and attempts to be in an area approximately 6 to 8 feet back of the short line and about 3 to 4 feet from the sidewall.

5. a. drive serve
   b. garbage serve
   c. lob serve
   d. Z-serve
   e. jam serve

6. The wrist is held in a cocked back position at the start of the stroke; at the moment of contact the ball is snapped or uncocked in order to impart the maximum power on the ball.

7. a. wall shot drill
   b. forecourt wall shot and crosscourt shot drill
   c. ceiling shot drill
   d. backcourt wall shot and crosscourt shot drill
   e. volley drill
   f. back wall drill
   g. kill shot
   h. overhead kill shot
   i. individual conditioning exercises

Index